M000014815

The Healthy Low Sodium Diet

Find out how to improve your health without losing the pleasure of eating and start your low-salt diet.

Alyson Brown

information. No warranties of any kind are declared or implied. Readers acknowledge that the author is not engaging in the rendering of legal, financial, medical or professional advice. The content within this book has been derived from various sources. Please consult a licensed professional before attempting any techniques outlined in this book.

By reading this document, the reader agrees that under no circumstances is the author responsible for any losses, direct or indirect, that are incurred as a result of the use of information contained within this document, including, but not limited to, errors, omissions, or inaccuracies.

Table of Contents

Introduction

You know that you've had a problem for long enough and that you are fed up with it. Whether it has been days, weeks, or months, you know that you have a problem that you cannot solve by sitting around and doing nothing. Your first step was to purchase this eBook. Your next step? To take another step forward, pay attention to - really pay attention to - everything that you read going forward. If you ever want to transform your life and embrace an entirely new lifestyle, then today is the day. You just have to take that first step.

As evident by the title of this eBook, you have been suffering from a poor diet that is filled to excess with sodium and extra salt, and you want to make a change, starting now. You know what your problem is. Whether you are suffering from acute kidney disease, high blood pressure, heart failure, edema, or some other condition, you know that the only way to solve your problem and transform your life is to embrace a reduced-sodium, low or no added salt diet. This might seem scary at first. After all, most of our favorite snacks and meals are filled with extra salt and increased levels of sodium—that is what makes it taste so good. That is what our brains remember when we take a bite into a greasy burger and salted crispy fries. We remember the salty grease and the savory crispiness of the French fries that we ate for our meal. We want more. We always want more. And we live in an age where products like meat and salty junk food are easily attained for a relatively reasonable price.

It is difficult and almost unthinkable, in the world we live in today, to sit back and say, "No thank you, I already packed my lunch" when a group of your coworkers asks if you want to get something from the local fast food restaurant that is housed just across from your work building. It's even more unthinkable to actually *mean it* and not regret your decision.

Some people may never reach that clarity, but it is my hope that you will do so through the creation of this eBook. You have already taken the first step in acknowledging that you have a significant health problem that means you need to (more than likely) overhaul your diet and get rid of the majority of your favorite foods and snacks. Perhaps you have to learn how to cook as well. I promise you, it is not even remotely as scary or complicated as it may seem at first. All you have to do is follow this guide, along with the meal plans that I have prepared for you, at the start of your journey.

No matter how well you fare in the kitchen, whether you burn water or use enough salted butter to make even the most talented French pastry chef cry, my hope is that you come away from this eBook not only learning a little bit more about how your new diet and lifestyle will affect your life and overall health until the end of your days, but I also hope to introduce you to some of my personal favorite recipes, as well as different spice blends and interesting combinations that you may not have thought to put together before. I hope to inspire you to learn how to budget and create your own meal plan, mixed and matched with favorites that you perhaps found in this eBook, but with a personal twist that could only come from you.

Even if you are not that great at cooking and you only learn how to cook exactly what you are shown in this eBook, I promise you that you will not regret this new direction that you have taken in your life. You have everything to gain and nothing to lose in embracing this new reduced sodium, low or no salt diet. It might be difficult at first. You may feel overwhelmed and stressed out, particularly if you are not used to spending time cooking. I promise you that as soon as you get comfortable with using different spices and cooking your own food, you will wonder why you hadn't done this before!

So, I hope you enjoy this eBook and the meal plans that I have enclosed within it. I hope I have helped clarify any questions you may have had, and that I've directed you to a whole eBook full of fun recipes that should be eaten and prepared with joy, by someone who is becoming a better, healthier person every time they start to prepare a meal.

Chapter 1: Understanding Your Diagnosis

Why a Low Sodium and Salt Diet?

When you have been given a diagnosis, it can seem like the scariest thing in the world, and it may be something you find yourself not wanting to face. However, the first step to living a better, healthier life is to accept what you cannot change. And right now, for whatever reason, you have to reduce the amount of sodium and salt you consume in your diet. Luckily, with a few tips and new skills, this can be something that creates a positive, profound change in your life. The first step is accepting what you cannot change—but the next step is finding out as much information as you can about your condition.

What conditions lead to a reduced-sodium and salt diet? Unfortunately, the most common conditions that require a low sodium diet include kidney disease, heart failure, and high blood pressure (Kubala, 2018).

If you have kidney disease, then you will already have some understanding that your kidneys are unable to excrete enough of the extra sodium or fluid in your body, which is why you have to limit your sodium intake. If you don't, and you continue to allow your sodium and fluid levels to be elevated, then your blood pressure will rise significantly higher and damage your kidneys (Kubala, 2018).

If you have heart failure, then you will already have some understanding that your heart, as well as your kidneys, are severely impacted. However, when your heart's normal functions are impacted, that leads to water and sodium retention, which can raise your blood pressure and cause shortness of breath as well (Kubala, 2018).

If you have high blood pressure, then you will already have some understanding that not only are you in danger due to your blood pressure, but you have already increased your risk of developing other conditions, such as a stroke or heart disease (Kubala, 2018).

These conditions are only the tip of the iceberg. If you do not reduce your sodium intake before it is too late, then you might find yourself developing more chronic, long-term conditions that cannot be fixed by diet alone. In order to combat these conditions, you next have to understand that it is not just about "reducing" your salt and sodium intake in terms of how much salt you add to your food.

It is also about flat out changing the foods that you eat. If you are someone who relies heavily on fast food, you will have to stop that immediately. If you are someone who relies heavily on premade sauces and salad dressings in your cooking, you will have to stop that immediately. Fast food, sauces, and salad dressings contain the highest sodium levels of anything you could possibly eat.

It might seem difficult at first, but all it takes is a little bit of practice and an open mind. If you have not done much cooking before, you may feel like a whole new world has opened up as you discover the power of herbs and spices. Remember, if you take this diet seriously, over time it will get easier and you will find yourself discovering new tastes and smells that you'd never cared for before. All without high levels of sodium and extra salt.

How Can a Low Sodium and Salt Diet Help You?

When you think of sodium in your diet, particularly added sodium, more than likely the first thought that pops into your head is table salt. Unfortunately for you, table salt is the least of your worries when it comes to added sodium, although it certainly is the easiest sodium level to control.

Sodium is necessary. While it is present in salt, which is a seasoning that most people love, it is also very helpful to your body. Without sodium, our bodies would not be able to regulate our fluids, keep our electrolytes balanced, keep our cells functioning, or maintain our blood pressure (Kubala, 2018).

To start your new lifestyle, you will need to limit your sodium to less than 2,300 mg (2.3 grams) of salt, which is around 2 teaspoons of salt a day (Kubala, 2018).

Do not think of your new lifestyle change as a restriction or a *diet*. Think of it as a return to what you should have been eating all along. Imagine if you had always eaten a bowl of chocolate ice cream with caramel syrup, whipped cream, and Oreo cookies on top every single morning for breakfast. And every single afternoon, you were sick to your stomach. Until one day, you decided to stop eating that giant bowl of ice cream with all of those toppings. You may have craved the ice cream later, but you didn't feel physically sick. You were going back to normal.

Think of your new low sodium diet as a method of reverting back to your body's actual needs, in terms of sodium levels. Most people consume far more sodium (and salt) than they need for their bodies to function properly. Without proper levels of sodium, your body cannot regulate the amount of fluid you have in your body, contract your muscles, send out nerve impulses, and regulate your blood pressure (Mozaffarian, n.d.).

Chapter 2: Eat Well to Live Well

Components of a Healthy Diet

A Balanced Diet

Having a balanced diet isn't just reflected on your outside, for example, if you are muscular and/or athletic, but also on your inside. Your body can focus on running itself in peak condition instead of suffering from hypertension, obesity, cancer, diabetes, depression, and heart disease—you may recognize a few of these conditions that can be caused solely having sodium levels that are too high ("Diet", 2016).

But what does a balanced diet look like? How can you know what a balanced diet looks like if you are so used to eating processed foods regularly? It can be difficult, especially at first, but the longer you stick with it, the more knowledge you will gain, and the more comfortable you will become with these changes.

The keyword in the phrase *balanced diet* is just that—*balanced*. That means that we have several components that make up a healthy diet, and while our bodies may need one component more than the other, that doesn't mean that it is better than the other, "lesser" component. It's just not what our body needs. Food does not have a moral value, but it does have *nutritional* value. And it's up to us to fulfill each value to its individual needs vs. our own wants and desires.

To maintain a balanced diet, what you need to consume are carbs, fat, vitamins, fiber, minerals, protein, and water ("Diet", 2016).

To maintain a balanced diet, you need to make sure that 45 to 55% of your daily calorie intake comes from carbs. You can get this through eating wheat, rice, corn, pasta, potatoes, and fruit/sugar ("Diet", 2016).

In a balanced diet, you will also need to make sure that 20 to 35% of your daily calorie intake is fats. You can get this through nuts, dairy products, and oils ("Diet", 2016).

Obtaining enough vitamins to satisfy a balanced diet is a bit more complex. You will need to make sure to eat a wide variety of nuts, vegetables, and lean meats to get enough vitamins, with each range being specific to the vitamin itself ("Diet", 2016).

Another important component of a balanced diet is fiber. You will need to make sure that you eat enough fiber through vegetables, fruits (mainly fruits), oats, and seeds to maintain bowel health and function ("Diet", 2016).

In maintaining a balanced diet, you can't forget about proteins as they are another vital macronutrient. You should make sure that 10 to 35% of your daily calorie intake comes from proteins. You can get this through meat, soya, fish, eggs, and beans ("Diet", 2016).

Finally, to maintain a balanced diet, you will also need to keep yourself hydrated with water. As the old saying goes, if you feel thirsty—you're already dehydrated!

Maintaining Your Sodium Levels

Part of maintaining a healthy diet and a healthy body is properly maintaining your sodium levels. When your levels are not maintained properly, you could suffer from hyponatremia or hypernatremia.

Hyponatremia

Hyponatremia literally means that the sodium levels present in your blood are too low. One of the ways that you can develop this condition—which causes your body's cells to swell—is by drinking too much water. In more serious, life-threatening cases, you will have to receive electrolyte solutions intravenously ("Hyponatremia", n.d.).

If you suspect that you have hyponatremia, look for the following symptoms: muscle weakness or cramps, confusion, vomiting/nausea, low to no energy, constant fatigue, and headaches. Watch out for these symptoms, particularly if you start vomiting, cramping, and have frequent headaches ("Hyponatremia", n.d.).

There are several causes behind hyponatremia. The most common cause is drinking too much water, which overwhelms the kidney's function to excrete water vs sodium, but there are several other causes you may be familiar with—congestive heart failure, kidney failure, severe dehydration through excessive vomiting and/or diarrhea, and the use of any anti-diuretic hormones. All of these causes will ensure that your body holds onto the fluid it has already filtered so that it stays in your body ("Hyponatremia", n.d.).

This condition has two stages. The chronic version can sneak up on you over a period of 48 hours, and mainly gives you moderate symptoms. However, the acute version occurs all at once, causing your sodium levels to drop almost instantaneously. If you are not careful, your brain could swell and this could even be fatal ("Hyponatremia", n.d.). Pay close attention to any symptoms you may have experienced in the past as you begin your journey to a healthier life.

Women who are close to the perimenopausal stage seem to be at a much higher risk of hyponatremia, as their sex hormones are linked to how the body balances sodium levels ("Hyponatremia", n.d.).

Hypernatremia

Hypernatremia literally means that the sodium levels present in your blood are too high. Sometimes you can get away with mild hypernatremia, without affecting your health (McBean, 2017). However, if you do not get it under control you could end up in serious trouble.

If you suspect that you have hypernatremia at any moment, look for the following symptoms: lethargy (usually presenting as low to no energy and severe fatigue), extreme thirst, and, sometimes, confusion. In more rare cases, you may suffer from spasms e.g. muscle twitching. This is due to the fact that your sodium levels influence how your nerves and muscles work (McBean, 2017).

You will have a higher chance of developing hypernatremia if you already suffer from diabetes, kidney disease, dehydration, vomiting, diarrhea (if it is watery), and several other conditions (McBean, 2017).

Be careful—hypernatremia is an acute condition that can strike you within a day. The most important aspect of treatment is to correct the sodium and fluid balance in your body. More than likely, your fluid intake will be increased and then your sodium levels will be checked. Also, something to consider— hypernatremia is usually an underlying condition and a symptom of a bigger problem (McBean, 2017).

Chapter 3: In Which Foods Is Sodium Present?

Foods with High Levels of Sodium

As stated earlier in this eBook, your daily sodium intake should be closer to 2,300 mg (or 2.3 grams) or 1 teaspoon of salt a day. This is particularly important to abide by if you suffer from heart disease, high blood pressure, or kidney failure.

However, there are several foods that are naturally high in sodium that you should avoid, or consume less of, and there are also foods that contain a surprising amount of sodium that perhaps you had never considered as a significant source of sodium. The following is a general list of sodium high foods, however, when you buy any food product you should read the label or use an online search engine to figure out how much sodium is in what you're holding, per serving.

Per serving is key. One fried chicken mini drumstick could have 1,150 mg of sodium, which would appear to be good as that is exactly half of the amount of sodium you should (generally) be consuming. However, a mini drumstick is barely larger than your thumb and there is no way you would only eat *two* of those as a meal.

Shrimp

The first surprising addition - shrimp. Even if you buy plain shrimp in the frozen packages, you still need to read the nutrition information. Often, "plain" frozen shrimp is actually lightly salted and then bathed in sodium heavy preservatives before the freezing process. A 3-ounce bag could contain as much as 800 mg of sodium. If you have the choice, go for freshly caught shrimp, or buy frozen shrimp that does not have salt additives (McCulloch, 2018).

Ham and Sausage

Sausage is naturally very fatty, so it is no surprise that it leads the pack with 415 mg of sodium within 2-ounce servings. Another easy to see example is ham. Ham often ends up extremely salty and high in sodium because salt is used to preserve, cure, and flavor the meat. That is why for every 3-ounce serving of ham you get, you will be eating 1,117 mg of sodium (McCulloch, 2018).

Canned Soup and Meat

Any sort of prepackaged soup will often have a high percentage of sodium, the sodium is used as a component of the preservation process. Thankfully, you can buy reduced or sodium-free versions of ready (or nearly ready) made soup, but be careful not to pick up any full sodium versions accidentally. 1 serving size cup of canned or prepackaged soup could have as much as 700 mg of sodium (McCulloch, 2018).

Canned meats e.g. tuna, chicken, turkey have also been gaining a lot of attention due to the amount of sodium they've been found to contain. Some brands have used as much as 425 mg of sodium per 3 ounce/single serving, which is incredibly high (McCulloch, 2018).

Cottage Cheese

While cottage cheese is a wonderful source of protein and calcium, it is very high in salt compared to the other two. A regular ½ cup serving size is the equivalent of eating 350 mg of salt a day. You will not see any reduced or no-sodium versions of cottage cheese, as unfortunately the salt not only alters the taste and texture of the product itself but is also a preserving agent for the cottage cheese. However, it has been shown that if you run cold water over your cottage cheese, then you can reduce the amount of sodium present by around 60% (McCulloch, 2018).

Vegetable Juice

While it may seem extra healthy to you, commercially available vegetable juices are often some of the worst offenders for high sodium levels present in foodstuffs. Pay attention to the nutrition labels of what you're consuming, especially if you think it's healthy. It never hurts to double-check. The healthy vegetable juice that you are drinking might have 5 or 6 different kinds of vegetable juice in it, but it could also have 405 mg of sodium per serving and 3.5 servings in the entire bottle. If you still want to drink commercially available vegetable juice, make sure that you buy reduced-sodium versions. Legally, the sodium levels cannot be higher than 140 mg per serving (McCulloch, 2018).

Salad Dressing

While some salad dressing contains higher sodium levels due to salt actually added to the dressings themselves for flavor, the biggest culprit is the type of salad dressings that have additives with sodium in them e.g. MSG, disodium inosinate, etc. (McCulloch, 2018). Be careful of the salad dressing that you choose if you still buy them after reading this eBook. Always go with the reduced or sodium-free options if you can. Otherwise, be aware that the majority of salad dressings average between 304 mg per 2 tablespoon serving (McCulloch, 2018).

Broth and Sauces

As we have established, sodium is an ingredient not only used in preserving, but flavorings as well. However, the use of sodium as a flavoring has gone a bit too far, for far too long. For example, an 8-ounce serving of a simple beef broth contains 782 mg of sodium. To combat this, either make your own broth and sauces or buy explicitly marked low or reduced-sodium broths and sauces (McCulloch, 2018).

Canned Vegetables

Again, as part of the preservation process, canned vegetables have more than their own fair share of sodium, with an average ½ cup serving size containing 310 mg of sodium. Luckily, if you drain and then rinse your canned vegetables in cool water for a few minutes, then you can reduce the amount of sodium that you are eating by at least 23% (McCulloch, 2018). If you don't want to deal with the sodium issue at all, then you can buy fresh or frozen vegetables.

Chapter 4: What Consequences Result from an Excess of Sodium?

Consequences of Excess Sodium

As stated earlier in this eBook, when you have high levels of sodium, that means your body is taking in more sodium than it needs or can handle. A small amount of extra sodium won't make a big difference in your overall health, but very often these types of situations escalate. If you continue to consume an excess of sodium, then your sodium levels will continue to rise, and your taste buds will become used to the processed, over-salted foods. Eventually, it will all come out in your health.

Your health will always tell the tale when it comes to your sodium levels. Perhaps you suffer symptoms of hypernatremia, high blood pressure, kidney disease, or heart failure. You may not know what those symptoms are, per se, but you will understand that something is wrong.

Symptoms of Hypernatremia

As covered before, hypernatremia (higher than normal levels of sodium) provides you with several symptoms to hint at its existence, the first being extreme thirst. What you may not know is that this could get ugly pretty fast, if your case is severe enough. If you worsen and do not seek medical attention or change your diet, then you could have issues communicating or even end up not being able to get your own water (Lewis, 2018). The next symptom is confusion, and in the worst case, you can end up slipping into a coma. The confusion is an outward manifestation of your brain cells literally shrinking, as your brain cells are dehydrated (Lewis, 2018).

Diagnosis of this condition is usually straightforward—in a hospital setting, your sodium levels would be measured. If your levels are measured to be high, then you will be given water orally, and if your levels do not change after a certain period of time, further testing would be needed. However, the main treatment is just that-- introducing more fluids into your body. An acute (sudden) case of hypernatremia should settle itself within 24 hours. Otherwise, you will need an extended hospital stay (Lewis, 2018).

Symptoms of High Blood Pressure

High blood pressure occurs when the amount of blood that your arteries pump is elevated or when your arteries become too narrow. Your blood pressure rises, which can cause long-term stress to your artery walls, resulting in a stroke or heart attack. Unfortunately, you can go for years without any symptoms of high blood pressure, which is why it is vital that you change your diet now, even if you aren't currently experiencing any symptoms ("High Blood Pressure", n.d.).

As stated above, the vast majority of people who have high blood pressure do not experience any symptoms, that is to say, they do not experience any of the recognizable symptoms of high blood pressure. This is normal, even if your blood pressure is a record-setting high. However, some people have reported symptoms such as nosebleeds, shortness of breath, and headaches—however, these symptoms did not occur until shortly before the person experienced a stroke or heart attack ("High Blood Pressure", n.d.).

The best way to diagnose or monitor your blood pressure is to get your blood pressure taken regularly. You can even buy a blood pressure cuff to take home with you and take your own blood pressure. If you have a family history involving heart attacks or strokes, it might not be a bad idea to either get your blood pressure taken regularly if you do not already, or take it regularly yourself, as you start this new journey.

Symptoms of Kidney Disease

Kidney disease is more commonly known as acute kidney failure. This occurs when your kidneys are just not able to filter your blood anymore. The effect of your kidneys not being able to filter your blood anymore means that any waste that it would have filtered out previously, such as excess sodium, is trapped in your body. The majority of the time, kidney failure is irreversible, even in sudden cases ("Acute Kidney Failure", n.d.).

Symptoms of kidney disease are relatively straightforward—if you suffer from, first and foremost, a huge reduction in the amount you pee, although you can occasionally go normally, and fluid retention, particularly in your ankles, legs, or feet, then you may have kidney disease. Couple this with the following symptoms—fatigue, nausea, weakness, confusion, chest pain, shortness of breath, and so on ("Acute Kidney Failure", n.d.).

35

If you have ever suffered from kidney disease due to eating an increased level of high sodium foods over a long (or short) period of time, then the obvious treatment is to increase your fluid (water) intake. However, if your case is particularly difficult, then you may need to take your fluids intravenously, and perhaps take a diuretic to allow you to expel the waste (excess sodium) ("Acute Kidney Failure", n.d.). With a proper diet, this would not happen at all.

Symptoms of Heart Failure

Heart failure seems to be a dirty word among the three other symptoms or hints that may point to you having higher than healthy levels of sodium. Heart failure is categorized as the heart's inability to pump blood throughout the arteries and veins of your body at the same level it operated at previously. The only way that you can prevent heart failure is to control the risk factors that can lead to heart failure, which include diabetes, high blood pressure, coronary artery disease, and obesity ("Heart Failure", n.d.).

The symptoms that point directly at heart failure include edema (swelling in legs, feet, and ankles), fluid retention, shortness of breath whenever you change positions (lay down or sit up), fatigue, increased urinary output, and chest pain ("Heart Failure", n.d.).

Part of the diagnosis of heart failure includes checking whether or not you have high blood pressure ("Heart Failure", n.d.). High blood pressure is a great contributing factor to heart failure, and a reduction of sodium intake followed by an increased fluid intake is the only thing that will lower your blood pressure, and in turn, lower your chances of heart failure.

A Short message from the Author:

Hey, are you enjoying the book? I'd love to hear your thoughts!

Many readers do not know how hard reviews are to come by, and how much they help an author.

I would be incredibly thankful if you could take just 60 seconds to write a brief review on Amazon, even if it's just a few sentences!

Your review will genuinely make a difference for me and help gain exposure for my work.

Thank you for taking the time to share your thoughts!

Chapter 5: Low Sodium Water and Its Benefits

Benefits of Low Sodium Water

What is Low Sodium Water?

When you hear the term, "low sodium water", what does it make you think of? Obviously, it is rather self-explanatory—it is water that has a small, harmless amount of sodium present. Harmless, in the sense that it will not add much sodium to your overall diet ("Low Sodium", n.d.). The recommended intake for everyone is 2,300 mg (or 2.3 grams) of sodium a day. Legally, if any food or beverage product is labeled "low sodium", then it has to have less than 20 mg of sodium per serving ("Low Sodium", n.d.).

Most people don't care about the amount of sodium in their water. Those that do suffer from heart disease, kidney failure, high blood pressure, etc., are more than likely more focused on what they eat and

39

how much sodium or added salt it contains versus the amount of sodium that is present in their water. For people who have severe issues with sodium levels in anything and everything, including their drinking water, low sodium water is sorely needed.

Interestingly enough, while sodium is a natural element and natural addition to our drinking water and other things, it is usually only found in underground drinking waterways. Recently though, higher levels of sodium have been found in our groundwater, which leads to a conundrum ("Sodium in Drinking Water", 2018).

The higher levels of sodium present in the groundwater could have and more than likely did come from a wide variety of sources. If you live in an area where it snows and plows use road salt to cut down on some of the work, that is still salt. That still contains sodium, which eventually melts down the snow on the road, and then absorbs back into the ground, and back to the groundwater, until it is ready to be filtered for other contaminants and drank right from your sink. It also ends up in the water when water softeners are added to hard water in order to remove the chemicals. Fortunately, for the majority of people, if the sodium levels go up, then they have nothing to worry about because it's everywhere and it's not going to affect them ("Sodium in Drinking Water", 2018). Only if you are particularly sensitive to a high sodium diet (which will eventually happen no matter what), will you be stressed.

Benefits of Low Sodium Water

The greatest benefit of buying low sodium water is obviously that you are ensuring that you are not consuming more than 20 mg of sodium at a time. If you have to watch your sodium water to that extent, then drinking the low sodium water is a godsend.

Until our society and culture transform into something different, we will never stop being surrounded by an increasingly fast-paced world. Until then, we will continue to find sodium wherever we turn to. No matter what we eat, drink, inhale, and consume, there is more than likely a significant amount of sodium in it. Even in healthy, untouched foods like fresh fruits and vegetables, dairy, meat, etc. The amount of sodium is low, but it is still present ("Salt and Sodium", n.d.). The addition of low sodium water to these ranks is somewhat akin to the first created diet soda, in one sense.

Our groundwater is being contaminated through man-made actions and while the increased sodium levels might not affect most of us, they do affect one too many people. It seems silly and somewhat hilarious to think that water could have such an effect, but if you live in a particularly horrible area in terms of drinking water, or have to monitor your blood pressure as well as your drinking water to start with, it would be enough to drive anyone mad.

While low sodium water can be a great addition to your diet, you should first and foremost focus on what you can control and what you can make changes to. If you feel that you need to, particularly if you live in a badly contaminated groundwater area, then using low sodium water might be the best way to go. It certainly could not hurt. But it should kick start the rest of your diet and lifestyle changes.

Sodium, particularly excess sodium and salt are especially present in the following foods: bread, sandwiches, cold cut meat/cured meat, pizza, burritos, tacos, snacks, chicken, eggs, cheese, and eggs ("Salt and Sodium", n.d.).

So, the best benefit of using low sodium water is that it can be your first step forward in your new lifelong, lifestyle change. It does not matter what brand you use, so long as you drink water that is low sodium e.g. contains less than 20 mg of sodium per bottle.

Chapter 6: Meal Plans

Snacks

Roasted Chickpeas

This snack is a great alternative to munching on peanuts, almonds, or walnuts, which often contain a lot of added salt.

Ingredients
- 16 ounces of canned, no salt added chickpeas, rinsed and dried
- 2 tablespoons of canola oil
- 4 tablespoons of brown sugar
- 4 teaspoons of chili powder
- ⅓ teaspoon of salt
- 1 teaspoon of garlic powder
- 1 teaspoon of onion powder

Directions
1. Preheat your oven to 350 degrees Fahrenheit.
2. In a medium bowl, mix the brown sugar, onion powder, garlic powder, salt, and chili

powder together. Add the chickpeas to the bowl and stir until they are evenly coated.

3. Place foil on a baking sheet and add the coated chickpeas in an even layer to the baking sheet. Bake for 1 hour or until the chickpeas are nicely browned.

This recipe makes 8 servings.

Granola Bars

Make your own savory-sweet granola bars at home by adding your favorite dried fruit, nuts, and peanut or almond butter combinations.

Ingredients
- 2 ¾ cups of rolled oats
- 1 ¼ cups dried coconut, shredded
- 1 cup of plain walnuts
- 1 cup of plain almonds
- 1 cup of plain peanuts
- ½ cup of honey
- ½ cup of coconut oil
- 2 tablespoons of lemon juice
- ½ cup natural peanut butter or almond butter
- 3 teaspoons of cinnamon
- 2 teaspoons of ground ginger

Directions

1. Preheat your oven to 350 degrees Fahrenheit.
2. In a large mixing bowl, add your oats, coconut, walnuts, almonds, and peanuts together. Mix until they are evenly dispersed.
3. Meanwhile, in a small saucepan, add the honey, coconut oil, lemon juice, natural peanut butter, cinnamon, and ginger together. Whisk until evenly mixed. Turn the heat to medium-high until it boils and then reduce it down to medium. Allow it to simmer for 5 minutes or until thickened.
4. Add the honey mixture to the oats and mix until the oats are completely coated.
5. Pour the honey-oat mixture into a greased baking dish, and then put into the oven to bake for 20 minutes or until firm. Do not slice until entirely cool.

This recipe makes 8 servings.

Beet Chips

A unique alternative to salty potato chips—don't knock them until you try them!

Ingredients
- 12 beets, sliced thinly
- 4 tablespoons of olive oil
- 1 teaspoon of salt
- 2 teaspoons of fresh rosemary, chopped

Directions
1. Preheat your oven to 375 degrees Fahrenheit.
2. In a small bowl, add the sliced beets, olive oil, rosemary, and salt. Mix together so that they are evenly coated.
3. On a cookie tray, arrange the beets in a single layer and place it into the oven to bake for 15 to 20 minutes.

This recipe makes 4 servings.

Lemony Fruit Salad

This fresh fruit salad features lemony jelly cubes to create a burst of citrus to cut down on the sweetness of the fruit.

Ingredients

- 1 cantaloupe or honeydew melon, diced
- 3 cups of fresh blueberries
- 3 cups of fresh strawberries, quartered
- 2 cups of plain yogurt
- 2/3 cup of white sugar
- 1 cup of water
- 1 tablespoon of gelatin
- ½ cup of lemon juice
- ¼ cup of water
- ½ cup of sugar
- Zest of 2 lemons
- Vanilla, to taste
- Fresh basil leaves

Directions

1. To make the yogurt jelly, coat a medium-sized baking dish with cooking spray and then line it with parchment paper or plastic wrap.
2. In a medium bowl, add ¼ cup of water and gelatin together and allow the gelatin to sit

for 5 minutes to soften. Set this aside in a dry bowl.

3. Get a small saucepan, add ½ cup of sugar, lemon juice, and lemon zest to boil over medium-high heat.

4. Add the gelatin and mix until the gelatin dissolves.

5. Take off the heat and then add the yogurt. Mix until it is completely enveloped and smooth.

6. Pour the gelatin-sugar mix into the prepared baking dish and then refrigerate for at least 5 hours, or until it is set firm. Slice the yogurt jelly into 30 cubes.

7. To make the syrup, add the vanilla, 1 cup of water, and ⅔ cup of sugar to a small saucepan. Mix until they are dissolved and then bring to a boil over medium-high heat.

8. Once the mixture reaches a boil reduce the heat back to medium and then allow it to simmer for a further 4 minutes.

9. Once the mixture has thickened, pour it into a different bowl and place in the refrigerator to cool down.

10. In a large serving dish, add all of the fruit and then pour the chilled syrup over the fruit, making sure that the fruit and syrup are evenly coated. Add the yogurt jelly and gently mix.

This recipe makes 8 servings.

Day 1

Breakfast: Yogurt and Rhubarb Compote

Start your day off with a light breakfast, complemented by an unusual fruit choice.

Ingredients
- 2 cups of rhubarb, chopped into bite-sized pieces
- ¼ cup of sugar
- ½ cup of water
- 3 cups of plain yogurt
- 3 tablespoons of honey
- 1 cup of plain sliced almonds

Directions

1. In a small saucepan, add the rhubarb, sugar, and water over medium-high heat. Bring to a boil, and then reduce to low heat, stirring

frequently. Keep over the heat until the rhubarb breaks down and is completely softened and starts to thicken into a sauce.

2. Pour into a glass bowl and place in the refrigerator to cool until completely chilled through.

3. In a mixing bowl, add the honey and yogurt together, mix until it is smooth.

4. Take 6 serving bowls out and spoon out equal portions of the yogurt-honey mixture.

5. Top the yogurt-honey mixture with rhubarb compote, and sprinkle with almonds. Enjoy chilled.

This recipe makes 6 servings.

Lunch: Pasta Vegetable Salad

Use any type of pasta to make this salad, including shells, rotini, or macaroni. Also experiment with flavored pasta e.g. tomato, spinach, or carrot flavorings, to add a new depth of flavor. Make this pasta in bulk for the upcoming week to save time.

Ingredients
- 12 ounces of macaroni pasta
- 25 ounces of unsalted canned tomatoes, diced
- 2 small white onions, diced

- 1 pound of mushrooms, sliced thinly
- 1 yellow bell pepper, sliced
- 1 red bell pepper, sliced
- 1 large zucchini, shredded and dried
- 1 tablespoon of olive oil
- ¼ cup of reduced-sodium chicken broth
- 1 tablespoon of garlic, minced (or garlic paste)
- 1 tablespoon of fresh basil, chopped
- 1 tablespoon of fresh oregano, chopped

Directions

1. Cook the pasta according to the package instructions.
2. Fill a large pot so that it is ¾ full of water, and bring to a boil.
3. Add the pasta and boil 8 to 10 minutes, or until the pasta is al dente. Drain the pasta immediately and add to a serving dish.
4. Coat in the pasta in olive oil evenly and set to the side.
5. Take a large skillet and add the chicken broth to heat up over medium-high heat.
6. Once it is heated through, add the onions, tomatoes, and garlic. Sauté the vegetables until the onions go translucent, for around 5 minutes.
7. Add the yellow pepper, red pepper, and zucchini to the skillet and sauté them until

they are crisp, for about another 5 minutes. Sprinkle with the basil and oregano.

8. Combine the pasta and the vegetable medley and mix gently together. Cover the pasta dish and refrigerate for at least 60 minutes before serving.

This recipe makes 8 servings.

Dinner: Vegetarian Chili

If you want to add some protein, like chicken or ground beef, go right ahead! Just dice and sauté a pound of your protein of choice until it is fully cooked and add it to the chili.

Ingredients
- 1 large white onion, diced
- 1 cup of celery, diced
- 2 green bell peppers, diced
- 2 tablespoons of garlic cloves, minced (or garlic paste)
- 2 quarts of unsalted canned crushed tomatoes
- 8 ounces of unsalted canned pinto beans, rinsed
- 2 tablespoons of cumin
- 1 tablespoon of black pepper

- 2 tablespoons of balsamic vinegar
- 1 tablespoon chili powder
- 1 tablespoon paprika
- 1 tablespoon of dried oregano
- 1 tablespoon of dried thyme

Directions

1. In a large stockpot, combine the onion, celery, garlic, bell pepper and 2 tablespoons of water over low heat. Cook for around 10 minutes, or until the onion goes translucent.

2. Add the crushed tomatoes, pinto beans, cumin, black pepper, balsamic vinegar, paprika, chili powder, dried oregano, and dried thyme. Cover the chili and allow it to simmer for the next 2 hours, stirring every 30 minutes. If the chili thickens too much for your tastes, add some water.

This recipe makes 8 servings.

Day 2

Breakfast: Quinoa Breakfast Bowl

Enjoy either a savory or sweetened version of this dish.

Ingredients
- 2 cups of uncooked quinoa, rinsed in cool water
- 4 cups of milk (or coconut milk if you prefer)

Savory ingredients:
- 1 cup of plain almonds
- 1 cup of plain walnuts
- 1 cup of peanuts
- ½ cup of all-natural unsweetened plain peanut butter
- ½ cup of all-natural unsweetened plain almond butter
- 2 eggs, scrambled with ½ teaspoon of salt and 1 teaspoon of black pepper
- Diced tomatoes, onion, and lemon juice

Sweet ingredients:
- 1 cup of Greek yogurt, honey-sweetened
- 1 cup of fresh blueberries
- 1 cup of apple, diced into bite-sized pieces
- ¼ cup of honey

Directions

1. In a large pot, add the milk over medium-high heat, stirring frequently until it begins to boil. Make sure that you do not burn the milk, and if you need to, reduce the heat.

2. Add the quinoa immediately and then reduce the heat to low.

3. Cover the pot and allow it to simmer for the next 10 to 15 minutes, or until the quinoa is completely cooked.

4. To create a savory quinoa dish, add any of the combinations of the following ingredients: almonds, walnuts, peanuts, peanut butter, almond butter, scrambled eggs, tomatoes, onions, and lemon juice.

5. To create a sweet quinoa dish, add any combination of the following ingredients: Greek yogurt, blueberries, apples, and honey.

This recipe makes 6 servings.

Lunch: Broccoli Rigatoni

Enjoy this light pasta salad as you continue on with your day!

Ingredients
- 1 pound of rigatoni
- 6 cups of broccoli (if frozen, thaw before use)
- 6 tablespoons of parmesan cheese, grated
- 6 tablespoons of olive oil
- 2 tablespoons of garlic, minced (or garlic paste)
- 2 teaspoons of black pepper

Directions
1. Prepare rigatoni according to package instructions. Using a large pot, fill it ¾ full of water and then bring to a boil. Add the rigatoni and boil for the next 10 to 12 minutes, or until the rigatoni is al dente. Drain immediately.
2. While you are cooking the pasta, add the broccoli to the boiling water. Cover the broccoli and boiling pasta for about 10 minutes, until the broccoli is fully cooked.
3. Quickly spoon the tender broccoli out of the boiling water, with a slotted spoon, into a bowl. If you have a steamer basket, you can use that instead of placing the broccoli directly into the boiling water.
4. Once the broccoli and rigatoni are cooked, pour into a covered dish, and coat with olive oil and garlic. Sprinkle the pepper and parmesan cheese on top. Serve warm.

This recipe makes 6 servings.

Dinner: Potato Soup

Enjoy the depth of flavor that the fennel adds to the soup. This isn't your average cream of potato soup!

Ingredients
- Fennel bulb, about 2 pounds, chopped
- 1 large red onion, diced
- 2 large red potatoes, peeled and diced
- 3 cups of no sodium added chicken stock
- 1 cup of milk
- 1 teaspoon of olive oil
- 3 teaspoons of lemon juice
- 3 teaspoons of fennel seeds, toasted

Directions
1. In a large stockpot, add the olive oil over medium-low heat.
2. Add the fennel and onion, increase the heat to medium-high. Sauté the fennel and onion until they soften, around 5 to 7 minutes.
3. Add the potatoes, milk, chicken broth, and lemon juice. Reduce the heat to low and cover the stockpot. Simmer the stock until the potatoes are tender, around 20 minutes.

4. Use a food processor to puree the soup until it becomes a smooth, even mixture. This can be achieved most easily in batches e.g. a single ladle at a time, depending on how large your food processor is.
5. Once the soup is pureed all the way through, reheat the soup until it is completely warmed.
6. Serve in individual bowls and sprinkle toasted fennel seeds on top.

This recipe makes 8 servings.

Day 3

Breakfast: Sweet Potato Donuts

This unique variation on a classic donut is perfect for an on the go breakfast. Make-ahead to save time.

Ingredients
- 1 cup of sweet potatoes, boiled and mashed
- 1 cup of dried cranberries, chopped roughly
- 8 cups of flour
- ½ cup of sugar
- 4 eggs

- 2 cups of milk
- ½ cup of shortening
- 3 teaspoons of active dry yeast
- 2 teaspoons of ground cinnamon
- 1 teaspoon of salt
- 4 tablespoons of water
- Oil for frying
- 1 cup of confectioner's sugar
- 3 tablespoons of apple cider
- Candy thermometer

Directions

1. In a mixing bowl, add 2 ½ cups of flour, sugar, cinnamon, salt, and yeast together and mix thoroughly.
2. In a saucepan, add the milk, water, and shortening over medium-high heat. Mix until just melted and dissolved together (at around 120 to 130 degrees Fahrenheit).
3. Add the milk mixture to the flour mixture and mix until completely incorporated smoothly.
4. Add the mashed sweet potatoes, eggs, and chopped cranberries. Add the rest of the flour and mix with a spoon, and then use your hands to knead just until the dough forms into a ball. Do not over-knead, you want this dough just mixed.
5. Place your dough in a greased container and cover with either a top or a towel. Set the

dough aside to rise for at least an hour, or until it doubles in size.

6. Flour a surface and tip the dough out onto the surface. Push the dough down with your fingers to knock back air and then roll it out to about a ½ inch thickness. Cut with a 2-inch donut cutter, or if you do not have one, use a cup of a similar circumference.

7. Place your cut donuts onto a greased cookie tray, at least 1 inch apart, and cover. Leave these donuts to rise for another 30 minutes or so, or until they double in size.

8. Using a large pot or deep fryer, add oil until it is about ¾ of the way full, and heat to 375 degrees Fahrenheit.

9. Take 2 to 3 donuts at a time, depending on the size of your fryer/pot, and fry them until they are nicely browned on each side, around 2 to 3 minutes each.

10. Place your newly fried donuts on paper towels so that the oil can drain.

11. To create a glaze, mix the confectioner's sugar with the apple cider and dip the donuts in the glaze. Allow them to set on a wire rack before placing them in a container. Store in the refrigerator.

This recipe makes 24 servings.

Lunch: Balsamic Pineapple Chicken Salad

Enjoy the vibrant flavor of this citrus-inspired salad.

Ingredients

- 4 boneless, skinless chicken breasts, cut into bite-sized pieces
- 8 ounces of unsweetened pineapple chunks, drained (reserve 3 tablespoons of the liquid)
- 2 cups of fresh broccoli, chopped
- 4 cups of fresh spinach
- 1 small red onion, thinly sliced
- 4 teaspoons of olive oil
- ¼ cup of olive oil
- 3 teaspoons of sugar
- 3 tablespoons of balsamic vinegar
- 1 teaspoon of cinnamon

Directions

1. To make the vinaigrette: In a small bowl add the vinegar, olive oil, pineapple juice, cinnamon, and sugar together and whisk until smooth. Set aside until later.
2. Using a large skillet, heat the olive oil over medium-high heat. Add the chicken, cooking to brown on all sides for around 10 minutes or less.

3. Once the chicken is finished cooking, place it into a serving bowl. Add the pineapple, broccoli, spinach, and onions. Toss together until it is reasonably mixed.
4. Pour the finished vinaigrette over the salad and toss again to coat evenly. Serve at room temperature.

This recipe makes 8 servings.

Dinner: Beef Brisket

This recipe is perfect for any tough cuts of meat you may have, as the high acidity levels in the additional ingredients tenderize the meat automatically, particularly if it is marinated overnight. Serve with potato salad or roasted root vegetables on the side.

Ingredients
- 2 ½ pounds of beef brisket, trimmed and sliced in 8 pieces
- 1 large white onion, roughly chopped
- 4 garlic cloves, peeled
- 14 ounces of no sodium added canned tomatoes, diced
- ¼ cup of white wine vinegar
- 1 cup of low sodium beef stock
- 2 teaspoons of dried thyme

- 2 teaspoons of dried basil
- 2 teaspoons of dried rosemary
- 1 teaspoon of black pepper

Directions

1. Preheat the oven to 350 degrees Fahrenheit.
2. In a large stockpot, add the teaspoon of olive oil along with the brisket at medium-high heat.
3. Add the pepper, thyme, basil, and rosemary to the brisket and mix.
4. Cook the brisket until it is browned on all sides. Remove the brisket after it has been browned to a nearby plate.
5. Add the onions to the large stockpot and cook until they are browned around 5 to 10 minutes.
6. Add the garlic and cook another 2 minutes.
7. Add the tomatoes (with the water), the stock, and vinegar. Mix and then add the brisket. Allow the mixture to reach a boil and then turn off the heat.
8. Put the stockpot in the oven and leave it in the oven for 3 to 3 ½ hours, or until the beef is tender and falling apart.

This recipe makes 8 servings.

Day 4

Breakfast: Apple Breakfast Salad

Here is another fruit salad that consists mainly of apples and bananas. Switch out the sunflower seeds with your favorite nuts, or the yogurt with a flavored but unsweetened variation.

Ingredients
- 2 large green apples, chopped into cubes
- 2 large bananas, thinly sliced
- 4 teaspoons of lemon juice
- ¼ cup of raisins
- 2 tablespoons of plain sunflower seeds
- 6 ounces of plain Greek yogurt
- 2 tablespoons of honey

Directions
1. In a serving bowl, add the green apples and bananas. Mix until they are evenly dispersed and then mix the lemon juice until it coats the apple-banana mix.
2. Add the raisins and sunflower seeds, mix again until evenly dispersed.
3. In a separate bowl, mix together the honey and Greek yogurt.

4. Pour the honey and yogurt mix over the apple-sunflower seed mixture until it coats the apple-sunflower mixture evenly.
5. Serve at room temperature.

This recipe makes 6 servings.

Lunch: Clam Fettuccine

Make this dish in advance and eat either cold or at room temperature for a refreshing pasta dish on the go.

Ingredients
- 10 ounces of fettuccine pasta
- 8 ounces of reduced-sodium canned clams, drained and rinsed
- 3 tablespoons of garlic cloves, minced (or garlic paste)
- 2 cups of corn (if frozen, thaw before use)
- 2 tomatoes, chopped and seeded
- 1 tablespoon of black pepper
- 1 teaspoon of salt
- 5 tablespoons of fresh basil, chopped
- 1 tablespoon of olive oil

Directions

1. To prepare the fettuccine pasta, follow the directions on the package. Or place a large pot filled to the ¾ mark full of water, and bring to a boil. Add the pasta and cook for 8 to 10 minutes, until it is considered to be al dente. Drain the pasta immediately.

2. In a medium-sized saucepan, add the tomatoes, garlic, corn, olive oil, wine, and fresh basil. Mix together and turn the heat up to medium-high. Stir frequently as it comes to a boil, and then reduce the heat and add the clams and fettuccine.

3. Cover the pot and simmer for another 3 minutes. Mix together thoroughly one last time, then sprinkle with salt and pepper.

4. Serve while still warm.

This recipe makes 6 servings.

Dinner: French Chicken

Enjoy this chicken with its creamy mushroom sauce. Add your favorite steamed veggies on the side to complete the meal!

Ingredients
- 8 chicken boneless, skinless breasts

- 8 shallots, sliced
- 1 pound of cremini mushrooms, sliced
- 2 tablespoons of garlic cloves, minced (or garlic paste)
- ½ cup of red wine
- 1 cup of reduced-sodium chicken stock
- 4 tablespoons of fresh rosemary, chopped (or 2 tablespoons of dried rosemary)
- 4 tablespoons of fresh basil, chopped (or 2 tablespoons of dried basil)
- 1 tablespoon of black pepper
- 3 tablespoons of dried thyme
- 2 tablespoons of flour
- 4 tablespoons of olive oil

Directions

1. Mix the black pepper and thyme together in a small bowl, set aside.
2. Pound the chicken flat between wax paper or cling film with a mallet or rolling pin. Coat the chicken in the black pepper and thyme. Cover and refrigerate.
3. In a saucepan, heat 2 tablespoons of olive oil above medium-high heat, and sauté the shallots until they are translucent.
4. Add the mushrooms and garlic. Cook for 4 minutes or until the mushrooms have softened and browned slightly.

5. Meanwhile, in a bowl, mix the flour and wine together smoothly, then add to the cooked mushrooms and shallots. Stir until mixed, then add the stock and stir occasionally until the liquid thickens. Reduce the heat and add the rosemary and parsley.

6. In a skillet, heat 2 tablespoons of olive oil over medium-high heat, and add the chicken. Brown both sides, for about 5 minutes on each side. Place chicken directly into the mushroom-shallot sauce and serve while hot.

This recipe makes 8 servings.

Day 5

Breakfast: Garlic Quiche

Who said eggs can only be seasoned by salt and pepper? Enjoy this quiche pie as a side to oatmeal or a light fruit salad.

Ingredients
- 15 ounce premade pie dough
- 3 eggs

- ¼ cup milk
- 6 ounces of cream cheese, room temperature
- 3 tablespoons of garlic paste
- 4 tablespoons of fresh chives, chopped
- 1 tablespoon of black pepper
- 1 teaspoon of salt
- 2 tablespoons of fresh parsley, chopped

Directions

1. Preheat your oven to 350 degrees Fahrenheit.
2. In a mixing bowl, add the cream cheese, garlic paste, chives, black pepper, salt, and parsley and mix until smooth.
3. Place the premade pie into the pie plate, and add the cream cheese mixture. Spread until it is completely even and smooth on top.
4. Place into the oven and cook for 20 to 25 minutes, or until the top is firm and slightly brown.

This recipe makes 8 servings.

Lunch: Lemon Salmon

Go back to the basics with this very simple dish, packed full of flavor.

Ingredients

- 8 salmon fillets
- 2 lemons, quartered (or 3 tablespoons of lemon juice)
- 1 tablespoon of fresh thyme, chopped
- 1 tablespoon of fresh basil, chopped
- 2 teaspoons of black pepper
- 1 large zucchini, chopped
- 8 ounces of cherry tomatoes, halved
- 1 small summer squash, diced
- Olive oil
- 1 teaspoon of black pepper
- 1 tablespoon of lemon juice

Directions

1. Preheat your oven to 350 degrees Fahrenheit. Prepare a cookie tray with cooking spray and foil.
2. In a bowl, coat the salmon fillets in olive oil and black pepper completely. Then add the fresh thyme and basil until the fillets are coated evenly.
3. In another bowl, add the zucchini, cherry tomatoes, and summer squash with 1 tablespoon of olive oil, 1 teaspoon of black pepper, and 1 tablespoon of lemon juice. Mix until thoroughly coated.
4. Arrange the fillets on the cookie tray so that they are laid out in a single layer, with enough

room to add the zucchini-lemon juice vegetable mix.

5. Squeeze the juice of 1 whole lemon over the fillets before you put them into the oven for 10 to 15 minutes, or until the flesh begins to flake in the middle.

6. Remove the fillets and leave the vegetables inside the oven until they are tender, for another 10 to 15 minutes.

7. Arrange the fillets and vegetables on 8 plates, squeeze the juice of 1 whole lemon on the fillets and serve.

This recipe makes 8 servings.

Dinner: Lebanese Chicken

Enjoy this traditional Lebanese twist on a classic American roast chicken and potato dinner.

Ingredients
- 8 boneless, skinless chicken thighs
- 8 red potatoes, quartered
- 4 tablespoons of garlic clove, minced (or garlic paste)
- ½ cup of olive oil
- 1 cup of lemon juice
- 1 teaspoon of salt

- 2 teaspoons of pepper
- 2 tablespoons of fresh basil, chopped
- 2 tablespoons of fresh parsley, chopped

Directions

1. Preheat your oven to 425 degrees Fahrenheit. Coat a large baking dish in cooking spray and set aside.
2. Prepare the chicken and potatoes, then add them to the baking dish. Sprinkle the salt and pepper over the chicken thighs and potatoes.
3. In a separate bowl, mix the basil, parsley, garlic, lemon juice, and olive oil together. Pour over the chicken thighs and potatoes, and ensure that they are equally coated.
4. Cover the baking dish with foil and put into the oven to bake for 30 minutes.
5. After 30 minutes, increase the heat to 475 degrees Fahrenheit, and roast the chicken and potatoes until they are crispy and browned.
6. Serve while still warm.

This recipe makes 8 servings.

Day 6

Breakfast: Purple Berry Smoothie Bowl

Enjoy this unusual twist on a power bowl.

Ingredients
- 12 ounces of plain Greek yogurt
- 2 cups of strawberries, frozen
- 1 medium banana, frozen
- 1 cup of blueberries, frozen
- 2 cups of spinach, fresh
- 1 cup of pomegranate juice
- 1 cup of orange juice
- 4 tablespoons of flaxseed
- 2 tablespoons of chia seed
- Fresh strawberries, blueberries, sliced bananas, oatmeal, or granola according to your preference

Directions
1. In your blender, add the Greek yogurt, bananas, strawberries, blueberries, spinach, pomegranate juice, and orange juice. Pulse until smooth.
2. Add the flaxseed and chia seed, then pulse a few times until evenly dispersed.

3. Evenly distribute the yogurt mixture into 6 bowls.
4. Top with your choice of strawberries, blueberries, bananas, oatmeal, or granola.

This recipe makes 6 servings.

Lunch: *Baked Herb Turkey*

Enjoy this recipe as a compliment to the fall season and upcoming holidays.

Ingredients
- 4 turkey breasts, cut in half
- 4 large yellow potatoes, quartered
- 2 tablespoons of olive oil
- ½ cup of water
- 1 tablespoon of dried sage
- 5 teaspoons of dried thyme
- 3 tablespoons of fresh parsley, chopped (or 2 tablespoons of dried parsley)
- 3 teaspoons of dried sage
- 1 tablespoon of dried thyme
- 3 tablespoons of fresh parsley, chopped (or 2 tablespoons of dried parsley)
- 3 tablespoons of honey
- ½ cup of apple juice
- Pan drippings

Directions

1. Preheat your oven to 325 degrees Fahrenheit. Prepare a cookie tray with cooking spray and foil.

2. In a small bowl, add 1 tablespoon of sage, 5 teaspoons of thyme, and 3 tablespoons of parsley together. Mix and set aside for later.

3. Rinse the turkey breast halves and dry them well. Place them on the covered cookie tray and gently separate the skin from the flesh.

4. Rub ½ of the prepared herb mixture you made earlier on each turkey breast, under the skin. Next, coat the turkey breasts in olive oil.

5. Place the potatoes and the turkey breasts onto the cookie tray.

6. Place the turkey in the oven and bake for around 60 to 90 minutes.

7. After the first hour, cover the turkey breasts in foil to keep them from drying out.

8. If the juices do not run clear or if the internal temperature isn't 170 to 175 degrees Fahrenheit, put the turkey back into the oven to cook a little longer.

9. When you have removed the turkey breasts and potatoes from the oven, place them on a serving platter and cover with foil. Let them sit for at least 20 minutes to allow the juices to reabsorb into the meat.

10. Get a medium saucepan and place it over medium-high heat. Add 3 teaspoons of sage, 1 tablespoon of thyme, 3 tablespoons of parsley with the honey and apple juice. Add the scrapings off of the cookie tray, as well as ½ cup of water.
11. Mix thoroughly and then reduce to medium heat. Simmer the liquid until it reduced halfway down and then starts to thicken.
12. Serve the turkey breasts with gravy and the baked potatoes.

This recipe makes 8 servings.

Dinner: Peppers and Cheese Ravioli

If you still crave pasta but are tired of eating tomato sauce, this recipe is perfect for you.

Ingredients
- 16 ounces of cheese ravioli
- 1 small yellow onion, diced
- 1 yellow bell pepper, sliced
- ½ green bell pepper, sliced
- 1 red bell pepper, sliced
- 2 cups of reduced-sodium chicken broth
- 4 tablespoons of olive oil
- 1 teaspoon of cayenne pepper

Directions

1. Prepare the ravioli according to package instructions. Or, fill a large pot ¾ of the way full of water and bring to a boil. Add the ravioli and boil for 8 to 10 minutes until tender. Drain immediately and set to the side.

2. Take a large skillet and place it over medium-high heat. Add olive oil, onion, yellow bell peppers, red bell peppers, and green bell peppers. Sauté them together until they are softened, around 5 minutes.

3. Add half of the broth and the cayenne. Reduce the heat to medium-low and simmer for another 5 minutes, and then add the rest of the broth. Continue to simmer and stir until the broth reduces further.

4. Spoon the ravioli into individual dishes and divide the pepper-onion mix on top of it.

This recipe makes 6 servings.

Day 7

Breakfast: Fruit Granola Bowl

Make this granola bowl as a healthy substitute for sugary cereal, and enjoy with your favorite nut or coconut milk.

Ingredients
- 5 cups of rolled oats
- 1 cup of unsalted almonds, sliced
- ½ cup of unsalted peanuts
- ½ cup of unsalted sunflower seeds
- ¼ cup of unsalted pecans, roughly chopped
- ¼ cup of unsalted hazelnuts, roughly chopped
- ¼ cup of raisins
- ¼ cup of cranberries
- ½ cup of brown sugar
- ½ cup of honey
- ½ cup of orange juice
- ¼ cup of canola oil
- 2 teaspoons of vanilla

Directions
1. Preheat the oven to 325 degrees Fahrenheit. Prepare a large baking dish or cookie tray by

spraying it with cooking spray and then covering it with foil.

2. In a small saucepan, add the brown sugar, honey, oil, and orange juice. Dissolve the mixture over medium heat and stir continuously. Remove from direct heat and add the vanilla. Stir until dissolved. Set aside.

3. In a large mixing bowl, add the rolled oats, almonds, peanuts, sunflower seeds, pecans, and hazelnuts. Mix until evenly dispersed together. Pour the slightly cooled brown sugar mixture over this mix until the oat mixture is completely coated evenly.

4. Pour the oat-brown sugar mix onto the prepared dish, making sure that the oats are smoothed evenly into the dish. Bake for 35 minutes, or until the oats are crisp. Stir every 10 to 15 minutes.

5. Cool the tray on a wire rack. Once the oats are completely cool, add the cranberries, making sure to evenly mix them in.

6. Store the granola in an airtight container and leave at room temperature, if you prefer. Serve with your favorite milk or added fresh fruit.

This recipe makes 8 servings.

Lunch: Pork Medallions with Carrots

Enjoy this straightforward meal on a leisurely day.

Ingredients

- 24 ounces of pork tenderloin, sliced into 8 pieces
- 32 ounces of carrots, peeled and roughly chopped
- 1 tablespoon of black pepper
- 2 teaspoons of dried thyme
- 2 teaspoons of dried marjoram
- 2 teaspoons of dried basil
- 2 teaspoons of dried fennel
- 2 teaspoons of dried sage
- 2 teaspoons of dried rosemary
- 2 cups of white wine

Directions

1. Pound the pork tenderloin flat between two pieces of waxed paper using a mallet or a rolling pin. Sprinkle the pork with black pepper, thyme, marjoram, basil, fennel, sage, and rosemary and allow it to rest for 10 minutes before frying.
2. In a large skillet, add the pork and olive oil. Cook over medium-high heat until the pork is nicely browned on both sides. This will be

around 3 minutes of cooking on each side. Once the pork is cooked, place in a covered dish to keep the pork warm.

3. After the pork is finished cooking, add the wine to the pan, allow it to reach boiling point. Continuously stir and scrape the pan, then add the carrots, reduce the heat to medium-low. Cover to cook for 5 to 10 minutes, until the carrots are tender. Spoon the carrots and the pork onto individual plates.

This recipe makes 8 servings.

Dinner: Tamales

Enjoy this classic Mexican cuisine. Make-ahead during the week to enjoy even further.

Ingredients
- 24 dried corn husks
- 36 ounces of boneless, skinless chicken breasts
- 1 large white onion, diced
- 1 yellow bell pepper, roasted and diced
- 1 red bell pepper, roasted and diced
- 2 celery stalks, diced

- 4 tablespoons of garlic cloves, minced (or garlic paste)
- 4 cups of reduced-sodium vegetable stock (you can use chicken as well)
- 4 teaspoons of black pepper
- 1 tablespoon of ground cumin
- 1 tablespoon of dried oregano
- 1 cup + 4 tablespoons of cornmeal

Directions

1. Soak the corn husks in water for at least an hour before using them.
2. Preheat your oven to 375 degrees Fahrenheit.
3. In a large skillet, sauté the chicken breasts in olive oil over medium-high heat until they are browned on both sides, at least 2 minutes per side. Remove from the skillet and set on a plate.
4. Add the white onion, yellow bell pepper, red bell pepper, and celery to the skillet and sauté for another 10 minutes, or until the vegetables are tender and browned. Add the garlic and sauté for another 2 minutes.
5. Put the chicken back into the skillet with the vegetables and add the stock, black pepper, ground cumin, and oregano. Cover the skillet and allow it to simmer for the next 20 to 30 minutes, or until the chicken is tender.

6. Remove the chicken and place it back on the plate to cool. After it is cool, pull it apart. Remove the vegetables and place in a bowl.

7. Meanwhile, add the corneal to the liquid leftover and put it over medium-low heat until the cornmeal absorbs the liquid. This creates masa.

8. Drain and dry the corn husks. Spread the masa-cornmeal mixture on the husks, then top with the vegetables and chicken. Roll the corn husk together to form a small burrito.

9. Place the tamales on a cookie tray and bake for 15 to 20 minutes. Serve while hot.

This recipe makes 8 servings.

Chapter 7: Low Sodium Recipes

Snacks and Appetizers

Potato Skins

While cooking with vegetables, we often find ourselves with leftover peels and other scraps. This recipe is a great way to use them instead of throwing them away.

Ingredients
- 4 small (or 2 medium) sized potatoes (we recommend either russet or sweet potatoes)
- 4 teaspoons of fresh minced rosemary (if you only have dried, use 2 teaspoons of rosemary)
- ½ teaspoon of black pepper, freshly cracked
- Cooking spray

Helpful Hint: These are only suggestions for you to build a base of flavor. You can add other spices, such as basil, chives, paprika, cayenne, cumin, etc. Don't be afraid to experiment with flavor. Once you start getting comfortable with it, you will find that you haven't even missed the salt in your meals.

Directions

1. Preheat your oven to 375 degrees Fahrenheit.
2. If you already have the skins prepared, simply wash them thoroughly. Otherwise, if you are working with whole potatoes, you will want to wash them, pierce them with a fork to allow the steam to come out, and then bake until the outside is crispy--at least an hour.
3. If you already have the potatoes peeled, then you should spray them with cooking spray, and then toss them with the spices. Put them in the oven, and keep a close eye on them. The cooking should take 30 to 35 minutes, depending on how thick the peels are. Periodically take them out to toss them and make sure the peels do not stick.
4. Serve hot. This recipe makes two servings.

Homemade Hummus

Homemade hummus is a great, low sodium filling to use either as a chip dip or in wraps.

Ingredients
- 4 large red bell peppers, roasted
- 4 cups of chickpeas (you can usually get these canned for easy use)
- 2 tablespoons of olive oil
- 2 tablespoons of lemon juice
- 2 teaspoons of cumin
- 3 teaspoons of garlic powder
- 3 teaspoons of onion powder
- ½ teaspoon of cayenne
- 1 teaspoon of salt
- 1 teaspoon of freshly ground black pepper

Directions
1. Cover a pan with foil to use.
2. Roughly chop and seed the red bell peppers. Arrange the peppers, skin side up on the pan and place in the oven.
3. Turn your broiler on and broil the peppers for 8 to 10 minutes, until the skins are nicely charred.
4. Once they are finished, take them out of the oven, and put them in a bowl with tongs.

Quickly cover them with foil for another 10 minutes to allow them to cook further via steam.

5. Open your cans of chickpeas and drain them.
6. After the peppers and chickpeas are prepared, add them, as well as the rest of the ingredients into a food processor and blend until smooth.

This recipe makes 8 servings.

Stuffed Mushrooms

Stuffed mushrooms are a great alternative to chips and dip, or any other unhealthy snack you may find yourself craving. They are also great as an appetizer at a party and can be made vegan, vegetarian, or omnivarian at a notice.

Ingredients

- 30 mushrooms (these can be any variety you enjoy, we recommend cremini or portabella mushrooms), that have been washed and stemmed

Topping

- 2 cups of bread crumbs (you can either buy these or make them by simply putting a few slices of bread through a food processor)
- ⅓ cup of unsalted butter, melted
- 2 tablespoons of parsley, freshly chopped (or 4 tablespoons of dried parsley)

Filling

- 3 cups of fresh basil leaves, chopped roughly
- 3 tablespoons of walnuts,
- ⅓ cup of parmesan cheese, grated
- 2 tablespoons of fresh garlic, ground (or you can buy already ground garlic)
- 2 tablespoons of olive oil
- 3 teaspoons of lemon juice

- 1 teaspoon of salt

Directions

1. Preheat your oven to 350 degrees Fahrenheit. Place your mushrooms on a baking sheet.
2. Create the topping by mixing together all of the topping ingredients (breadcrumbs, butter, parsley) into a separate bowl.
3. Create the filling by adding the basil leaves, walnuts, cheese, garlic, olive oil, lemon juice, and salt together in your food processor and process until mixed smoothly.
4. Spoon the filling into the mushrooms until they are full, then generously add the topping. Make sure you press down on the topping so it browns evenly in the oven.
5. Bake for 10 to 15 minutes, or until the topping is golden brown.

This recipe makes 30 servings.

Black Bean Dip

Ingredients

- 2 cans (31 ounces), or 4 cups of black beans, drained and rinsed thoroughly
- 8 small tomatoes (3 cups), diced and seeded (if you prefer)
- 2 cups of corn (frozen is fine, just thaw)
- 2 red or yellow peppers (your preference), chopped and seeded
- 1 medium red or white onion (your preference), diced
- 1 cup of parsley, chopped
- 4 garlic cloves (or 4 tablespoons of garlic paste)
- 1 tablespoon of sugar
- Juice from a lemon or 2 tablespoons of bottled lemon juice

Directions

1. Chop the tomatoes, peppers, onion, parsley, and garlic to your satisfaction.
2. Use a large bowl to mix all of the ingredients together, gently. You don't want to crush the tomatoes or beans.
3. This can be made up to an hour before you eat it, or allow it to rest and marinate in the refrigerator overnight for the best taste.

This recipe makes 16 servings.

Oven Roasted Potatoes

Oven-roasted potatoes are a staple that never gets old and is easy to make. This particular recipe cooks quickly because the potatoes are small.

Ingredients

- 1 ½ pounds of small red or white potatoes (your preference)
- 1 tablespoon of fresh rosemary, chopped (or 2 teaspoons of dried rosemary)
- 4 tablespoons of fresh parsley, chopped (or 4 teaspoons of dried parsley)
- 1 teaspoon of freshly ground black pepper
- ½ teaspoon of salt
- 2 tablespoons of olive oil
- 1 tablespoon of unsalted butter, melted
- 6 garlic cloves (or 3 tablespoons of garlic paste)

Directions

1. Preheat your oven to 400 degrees Fahrenheit. Choose either a baking dish or tray--cover in foil or cooking spray to prevent sticking.

2. Use a large bowl to combine your potatoes, garlic, rosemary, black pepper, salt, olive oil, and melted butter. If you want the potatoes to cook faster, you can cut them into halves or quarters.

3. Place your potatoes in your baking dish or tray in a single layer to ensure even cooking. Cover with foil or a lid before placing in the oven.

4. Bake for 25 minutes, then remove from the oven. Remove the foil or lid, and put back into the oven for a further 10 to 15 minutes until the potatoes have browned and softened to your satisfaction.

5. Once cooked, remove the potatoes from the baking dish or tray and move to a serving bowl. Sprinkle the potatoes with the parsley and gently toss to mix it evenly.

This recipe makes 8 servings.

Tomato and Mozzarella Salad

Tomato and Mozzarella salad is a salad that packs a lot of flavor in a few ingredients. Enjoy this fresh-tasting salad any time of the year, particularly in the spring and summer as the weather calls for it.

Ingredients
- 16 ounces of cherry tomatoes (you can use grape tomatoes if you prefer)
- 16 ounces of fresh mozzarella balls
- 20 basil leaves, fresh
- 2 tablespoons of olive oil
- 1 teaspoon of salt
- 2 teaspoons of black pepper

Directions
1. Gather your tomatoes and mozzarella balls. Cut them in half. If you cannot find mozzarella balls, then any water or whey packed fresh mozzarella is fine to use. Simply cut into bite-sized pieces. Place them in a medium-sized serving bowl.
2. Tear the fresh basil leaves into bite-sized pieces, around 2 or 3 pieces, depending on the size. Place in the bowl with the tomatoes and mozzarella. Add the salt, black pepper, and olive oil. Gently toss together.

3. Chill for 30 minutes or overnight for best results.

This recipe makes 10 servings.

Fresh Fruit Salad

This fresh fruit salad is perfect for ending a warm summer day--or perhaps to remind you of warmer weather as fall and winter approach.

Ingredients
- 8 ounces of pineapple chunks, canned
- 3 kiwis, peeled and sliced thinly
- 4 ounces of grapes, cut into quarters
- 3 bananas, sliced
- 8 ounces of strawberries, cut into quarters
- 3 teaspoons of lime juice
- 18 ounces of sugar-free yogurt, flavored in either lemon or lime
- 2 teaspoons of sugar

Directions
1. Cut the pineapple, kiwi, grapes, bananas, and strawberries as directed. Mix gently. Place in a medium serving bowl.
2. In a different, small bowl mix the yogurt, sugar, and lime juice together. Pour the

yogurt-sugar-lime mixture over the fruit and gently toss.

3. Chill before serving or eat directly.
4. If you want to, you could also buy wooden skewers to place the fruit on for personalized, individual servings for guests. Place the yogurt-sugar-lime mixture on the side for dipping.

This recipe makes 6 servings.

Black Eyed Peas

Black-eyed peas are a great side dish on their own— or you can add a protein or some cornbread to make it into a full meal! Use your favorite spices and herb additions to make it your own unique dish.

Ingredients
- 2 cups of black-eyed peas (low sodium canned or dried; if dried, you will need to soak them in water overnight to prepare them)
- 2 cups of unsalted canned crushed tomatoes
- 1 onion, diced
- 3 stalks of celery, diced
- 2 teaspoons of low sodium vegetable or chicken flavored bouillon granules OR 3 cups

of low sodium vegetable or chicken broth, for dried black-eyed peas

- 3 cups of water for the low sodium bouillon granules, for dried black-eyed peas
- 1 teaspoon of mustard, dry
- ½ teaspoon of ground ginger
- ¼ teaspoon cayenne pepper
- ½ teaspoon black pepper
- 1 tablespoon of garlic, minced (fresh or paste)
- 1 bay leaf

Directions

1. If you are using dried black-eyed peas, soak them overnight in 5 cups of water. Drain, then rinse. Afterward, place the black-eyed peas in a medium-sized pot. Add 2 cups of the water or broth to the black-eyed peas, and bring to a boil. Allow to boil for 4 minutes, then cover the pot, and let them stand for at least an hour off the heat. Then drain the water completely.

2. If you are using low sodium canned black-eyed peas, simply add to the pot as is.

3. Whichever method you use, add 1 cup of water and bouillon (or 1 cup of broth), tomatoes, celery, onion, garlic, cayenne, mustard, ginger, bay leaf, and black pepper. Mix thoroughly and then bring it to a boil.

4. Once the boiling point has been reached, cover it, and then reduce the heat to low, and allow the black-eyed peas to simmer for 1-2 hours, depending on if you used canned or dried black-eyed peas (dried black-eyed peas will require a longer cooking time).

5. Check every 20 minutes to make sure that the peas are still covered in liquid. Add water and bouillon or broth to keep them covered while cooking.

6. Place in a serving dish and serve.

This recipe makes 8 servings.

Artichoke Dip

You may consider artichoke dip to be an expensive, time-consuming recipe. Well, we are here to tell you that it is neither! Enjoy this dip at any time.

Ingredients
- 1 (15 ounce) can of artichoke hearts, rinsed and drained
- 8 ounces of white beans, unsalted
- 4 cups of fresh spinach, chopped
- 2 garlic cloves (or 2 tablespoons of garlic paste), minced

- 3 tablespoons of parmesan cheese, freshly grated
- 2 teaspoons of black pepper
- 2 teaspoons of fresh thyme (or 1 teaspoon of dried thyme)
- 4 teaspoons of fresh parsley (or 2 teaspoons of dried parsley)
- ½ cup of sour cream or plain Greek yogurt

Directions

1. Preheat your oven to 350 degrees Fahrenheit.
2. Combine all of the ingredients in a mixing bowl, and then place them in a lightly greased baking dish.
3. Bake for at least thirty minutes, or until the top is slightly browned. Serve warm, straight out of the oven.

This recipe makes 8 servings.

Main Meals

Roast Chicken

Chicken is one of the least expensive proteins you can buy at the grocery store, and what is so great about it is that it is very versatile. This recipe is perfect for busy parents or those just learning how to cook for themselves. Use the leftovers as a protein for a cold salad or another serving.

Ingredients
- 1 whole "roaster" chicken, about 7 pounds
- 2 garlic cloves, minced
- 2 tablespoons of fresh rosemary (or 1 tablespoon of dried rosemary), minced
- 2 tablespoons of fresh thyme (or 1 tablespoon of dried thyme), minced
- 2 tablespoons of fresh basil (or 1 tablespoon of dried basil), minced
- 1 tablespoon of onion powder
- ½ teaspoon of black pepper
- ½ teaspoon of salt
- 2 tablespoons of olive oil
- 4 sprigs of fresh rosemary, optional

Directions

1. Preheat your oven to 350 degrees Fahrenheit.
2. Mix together the minced rosemary, thyme, and basil with minced garlic.
3. Gently pull the chicken skin away from the flesh, and rub the chicken with the olive oil and the minced garlic mixture.
4. Mix the onion powder, salt, and black pepper together, and sprinkle over the top of the chicken.
5. If you choose to use the fresh rosemary sprigs, place them in the cavity of the chicken (after removing the organs, if they have not already been removed).
6. Truss the chicken by using twine to tie the legs and wings close to the body of the chicken, to ensure even cooking.
7. Put your chicken in a prepared roasting pan. The general rule of thumb states that you should roast each pound of chicken for at least 25 minutes, so roast your chicken for 175 minutes or 2 hours and 55 minutes. Take the chicken out every 30-40 minutes to baste with its own juices.
8. Check the internal temperature of your chicken—it should be at least 165 degrees Fahrenheit. The chicken should be browned, and its juices should run clear. Remove from

the oven and place on a serving dish to carve as you wish.

This recipe makes 8 servings.

Beef-Vegetable Skewers

Marinate the meat in this recipe overnight for more flavor not derived from salt!

Ingredients
- 1 ½ cups of rice (brown, if you have it)
- 6 cups of water, for boiling
- 12 ounces of sirloin (or any other beef product that you prefer)
- 2 green peppers, seeded and roughly chopped into 8 large pieces
- 12 cherry tomatoes, cut into quarters (seed, if you prefer)
- 2 medium onions, cut into quarters
- 3 tablespoons of low fat or fat-free Italian dressing (or your favorite salad dressing)
- 6 skewers (if wooden, soak in clean water for at least half an hour)

Directions
1. Use the 6 cups of water to make the rice. Place the rice and water in a pan on the oven. Bring

to a boil and then turn the heat on low, cover, and allow to simmer for the next 30 to 40 minutes, until the water is absorbed by the rice, and the rice is tender to eat. You may need to add more water, so keep an eye on your rice, especially if you are not used to making rice on the stove. If you have a rice maker, use that instead. Simply follow the instructions that go along with your machine.

2. Slice your beef into 12 equal pieces. Use a fork or knife to stab the meat, and then place it in a covered container. Pour your favorite salad dressing over it, making sure to coat every piece of meat thoroughly, and then put it into the refrigerator to marinate. If you are in a hurry, you can marinate your meat for 30 minutes, but for more flavor, marinate overnight.

3. To cook, you can either use your oven or grill. Whichever you choose, take the skewers and skewer the meat, onions, green peppers, and cherry tomatoes in an alternating style. Depending on the size of the meat, grill or broil your skewers in 5 to 10-minute intervals until cooked to your preferred temperature.

4. Serve with brown rice.

This recipe makes 6 servings.

Tarragon Chicken

Tarragon chicken is a fun twist on the roast chicken we all know and love, yet familiar enough to not scare off newcomers to the kitchen!

Ingredients

- 2 pounds of boneless, skinless chicken breasts
- 3 cups of pearl onions
- 3 cups of celery, chopped
- 1 tablespoon of fresh tarragon (or 2 teaspoons of dried tarragon)
- 2 teaspoons of black pepper
- 4 cups of chicken broth, unsalted or low sodium
- 1 ½ cups of wild rice
- 1 ½ cups of white rice
- 3 cups of white wine

Directions

1. Preheat your oven to 300 degrees Fahrenheit.
2. Using a large baking dish, combine both types of rice, broth (1 cup), and white wine together. Let it stand at room temperature for at least 30 minutes while you prepare the chicken.

3. Chop your chicken breasts into bite-sized pieces. Put them in a saucepan, along with the onions, tarragon, celery, and black pepper.

4. Sauté the chicken and vegetables over medium-high heat for around 10 minutes. Allow it to cool before proceeding with the next steps.

5. Add the vegetables and chicken to the baking dish with the rice and wine-broth. Cover it and bake for at least 1 hour. Check every 20 minutes, briefly, to see if you need to add more liquid to the rice.

6. Serve when it comes out of the oven.

This recipe makes 12 servings.

Asian Inspired Salmon

This is a fun, flavorful way to dress up a staple protein.

Ingredients
- 8 salmon fillets, around 4 ounces each
- 2 tablespoons of sesame oil
- 2 tablespoons of red wine vinegar (or rice wine vinegar, if you prefer)
- 2 tablespoons of reduced-sodium soy sauce

- 2 tablespoons of fresh minced ginger (or store-bought ginger paste)

Directions

1. Combine the sesame oil, ginger, vinegar, and soy sauce in a small bowl.
2. Place the salmon in a container with a cover, and coat the salmon with the sesame oil mixture. Make sure all sides of the salmon are coated and put it in the refrigerator for at least 1 hour before cooking it. If you like, you can leave it overnight for the best flavor.
3. To cook, either grill or sauté over medium-high heat in a saucepan. You should cook it for about 5 minutes on each side. You will know it is ready when the center flakes when you touch it with a fork or knife.

This recipe makes 8 servings.

Marinara Pasta with Vegetables

Spaghetti doesn't have to be full of meat and salt! The vegetables add extra body to the sauce, without any extra sodium or grease. Experiment with different flavor combinations to find your favorites!

Ingredients

- 16 ounces of spaghetti (whole wheat, if you can find it)
- 2 zucchini squash, sliced thinly
- 2 small white onions, diced
- 2 yellow summer squash (any squash you can find, or substitute for more zucchini), sliced
- 32 ounces of canned diced tomatoes, in water
- 15 ounces of plain canned tomato sauce
- 2 teaspoons of ground black pepper
- 1 teaspoon of sugar
- 2 tablespoons of minced garlic (or garlic paste)
- 1 teaspoon of salt
- 2 tablespoons of fresh oregano (or 3 teaspoons of dried oregano)
- 2 tablespoons of fresh basil (or 3 teaspoons of dried basil)
- 2 tablespoons of onion powder
- Olive oil

Directions

1. To make the sauce, place a medium saucepan over medium-high heat, and add 1 tablespoon of olive oil, garlic, and onion to the skillet. Sauté for a few minutes until the onions become translucent.

2. Add the zucchini and squash for further cooking, about 5 to 10 minutes more until they become softened.
3. Add the diced tomatoes, tomato sauce, black pepper, salt, sugar, oregano, onion powder, and basil. Reduce the heat and cover. Cook until the sauce has thickened, around 30 to 40 minutes.
4. To cook the pasta, use a large pot and fill it at least ¾ of the way with water. Bring it to a boil, and add the pasta. Cook for 10 to 15 minutes, until the pasta, has reached al dente. Drain before eating.

This recipe serves 8

Wild Rice with Squash

This recipe can be paired with any other type of squash e.g. pumpkin, butternut squash, zucchini, or eggplant. Find what's available in your local stores to make this recipe your own.

Ingredients
- 5 cups of winter squash, peeled and diced into bite-sized pieces
- Canola oil
- 1 ½ cups of white onion, diced

- 4 cups of wild rice, already cooked
- ⅓ cup walnuts, chopped
- 1 orange, peeled and segmented
- 1 tablespoon of parsley, chopped (or 2 teaspoons of dried parsley)
- 1 teaspoon of dried thyme
- 2 teaspoons of black pepper

Directions

1. To cook the rice, if you have a rice cooker, follow the directions there. Otherwise, place your 4 cups of uncooked wild rice in a pot, then add 8 cups of water.
2. Turn the heat to medium-high, and then wait for your pot to boil. Let it boil for 2 minutes, and then reduce the heat and cover.
3. Allow it to cook for the next 30 to 40 minutes, checking on it occasionally. If the water absorbs into the rice before it is fully cooked, then add more liquid. Otherwise, when the rice is fully cooked, drain any excess liquid.
4. Preheat your oven to 400 degrees Fahrenheit.
5. Coat the squash in canola oil and 1 teaspoon of black pepper in a small bowl. Using a roasting pan or tray, place your coated squash into the pan and place it in the oven. Roast for 35 minutes or until the squash has browned.

6. After your squash is cooked, use a medium-sized saucepan to sauté your onions in canola oil, until they are browned.

7. Add the squash, onion, orange, thyme, parsley, black pepper, and rice to your pan and sauté for another 5 minutes, stirring constantly.

This recipe makes 8 servings.

Fresh Veggie Polenta

This is a great meal for a lazy winter day, or it can be a side to a roast chicken or turkey.

Ingredients
- 2 cups of cornmeal
- 8 cups of water
- 2 tablespoons of minced garlic (or garlic paste)
- 2 cups of your favorite mushrooms, sliced (I recommend cremini, portobello, or button mushrooms)
- 1 large white onion, sliced thinly
- 2 cups of broccoli florets (if frozen, thaw them)
- 1 large zucchini, sliced
- 3 tablespoons of parmesan cheese, grated

- 1 tablespoon of fresh basil, chopped (or 2 teaspoons of dried basil)
- 1 tablespoon of fresh rosemary, chopped (or 2 teaspoons of dried rosemary)
- 1 tablespoon of fresh oregano, chopped (or 2 teaspoons of dried rosemary)
- Olive oil or cooking spray

Directions

1. Preheat your oven to 350 degrees Fahrenheit. Using your favorite cooking spray or olive oil, coat the inside of a large baking dish.

2. In a bowl, mix the water, polenta, and 1 tablespoon of the garlic together. Then add to the baking dish and place in the oven. It should bake for around 35 minutes, or until the polenta begins to pull away from the sides of the dish. Remove from the oven. Be careful not to overbake, as the polenta should be moist.

3. While you are cooking your polenta, take out a medium-sized saucepan and apply either the cooking spray or olive oil.

4. Add the onions with the other tablespoon of garlic and sauté for 2 minutes, until the onions are translucent.

5. Add the basil, rosemary, oregano, mushrooms, broccoli, and zucchini. Sauté

another 5 minutes, or until the vegetables are tender.

6. Once your polenta is finished, portion out the servings, then top with the vegetables and parmesan cheese.

This recipe makes 8 servings.

Roast Turkey

Use the leftovers for soup or sandwiches!

Ingredients

- 1 turkey, around 12 pounds
- 2 medium shallots, minced
- 6 garlic cloves, sliced thinly
- 3 carrots, roughly chopped
- 3 celery stalks, roughly chopped
- 2 medium yellow onions, roughly chopped
- 8 tomatoes (Roma or Oxheart, or your favorite brand)
- 1 tablespoon of dried thyme
- 1 tablespoon of dried rosemary
- 1 tablespoon of dried basil
- 2 tablespoons of black pepper
- 1 teaspoon of salt

Directions

1. Preheat your oven to 400 degrees Fahrenheit.
2. Combine the shallots, garlic, black pepper, salt, basil, rosemary, and thyme in a small bowl. Make sure it is mixed completely and set to the side.
3. Using a roasting pan, place your chopped carrots, celery, and onion in the bottom, evenly.
4. When you take out your turkey, remove the extras from the body cavity (the neck, giblets, and organs). You can save the neck to make stock if you want, otherwise, throw the rest of it away. Rinse the turkey out completely, then dry it.
5. Placing the turkey breast side up in the roasting pan, rub-down the turkey with the shallot mixture, you made earlier. Place your tomatoes around the turkey, and put inside the oven, uncovered.
6. You want to bake your turkey for 25 minutes at 400 degrees Fahrenheit, but then reduce the temperature down to 325 degrees Fahrenheit. Check on your turkey at around the 3 to 3 ½ hour mark. Its internal temperature should reach 170 to 175 degrees Fahrenheit, and its juices should run clear.

7. If you want to make stock with the turkey neck, simply put it in a saucepan, along with 4 cups of water, over medium-high heat. Once it reaches a boil, reduce the heat to medium, then allow it to simmer for around an hour. You can then either freeze this or use the stock to make turkey gravy.

8. Once your turkey is finished, remove it from the roasting pan and arrange it on a serving dish. Add the vegetables to the dish as well, and then cover with either a cover or aluminum foil for at least 25 minutes to allow the juices to soak back into the turkey before you carve it. Carve and serve.

This recipe makes about 12 servings, with plenty for leftovers.

Southwestern Veggie Bowl

Once you get the hang of this recipe, you can experiment not only with different vegetable additions but also with when to leave an ingredient raw or when to cook it.

Ingredients
- Canola oil
- 1 ½ cups red onion, chopped

- 3 cups green bell pepper, chopped
- 1 chili pepper, minced (optional)
- 4 garlic cloves, minced
- 1 ½ cups of sweet potato, peeled and diced
- 1 ½ cups of fresh tomato, chopped
- 1 ½ cups of brown rice
- ¾ cup of green lentils
- ¾ cup of red lentils
- 1 ½ cups of canned black beans, rinsed
- 5 cups of kale, chopped
- 3 cups of water
- 3 cups of low sodium or no salt vegetable stock
- 1 ½ tablespoon of white wine vinegar
- 2 tablespoons of ground cumin
- 2 tablespoons of black pepper
- 2 tablespoons of fresh cilantro, minced
- Lime wedges

Directions

1. Using a large saucepan, add the canola oil and turn the heat to medium-high.
2. Once it has heated through, add the onion, bell pepper, garlic, tomato, and sweet potato. Cook for around 15 minutes, or until the onions are translucent and the vegetables are tender.
3. Add the lentils, rice, vinegar, stock, water, cumin, and black pepper to the vegetable mix

and then bring to a boil. Once it has boiled for 2 minutes, reduce the heat and let it simmer for 45 minutes, covered.

4. Add the black beans, kale, and cilantro to serve individual portions.

5. Garnish with lime wedges in each bowl.

This recipe makes 9 servings.

Vegetable Pizza

This vegetable pizza is great, as you can use it as a base to add any type of veggie topping you want.

Ingredients
- Two 15-inch premade pizza crusts (your preference in the brand)
- 1 ½ cups of low sodium mozzarella cheese, grated
- 1 large purple onion, sliced thinly
- ½ cup black or green olives, sliced
- 2 large tomatoes (your preference), sliced
- 1 large yellow bell pepper, sliced
- 1 ½ cups of plain canned tomato sauce
- 1 tablespoon of dried basil
- 1 tablespoon of dried rosemary
- 1 tablespoon of dried thyme
- 1 tablespoon of dried parsley

- 1 tablespoon of onion powder
- 1 tablespoon of garlic powder

Directions

1. Roll out the pizza dough onto individual cookie trays. Preheat the oven according to the directions for the dough.
2. Mix the basil, rosemary, thyme, parsley, onion powder, and garlic powder together in a small bowl. Set aside.
3. Using a spatula, spread the plain tomato sauce over the pizza dough, evenly. Divide the herb mix into two bowls. Sprinkle each pizza with half of the herb mixture, then cover in cheese.
4. Add the vegetable toppings, and then sprinkle the rest of the herb mixture over the vegetables.
5. Bake according to pizza dough instructions.

This recipe makes 12 servings.

Beef Stew

This recipe is perfect for those days when you don't have a lot of time to cook. You can easily double or triple this recipe and place the extra portions in the freezer to be eaten later.

Ingredients

- 2 pounds of beef stew meat
- Canola oil
- 4 cups of white onions, diced
- 2 cups of celery stalks, diced
- 2 cups of tomatoes, diced
- 1 cup of potatoes, diced
- 1 cup of sweet potatoes, peeled and diced
- 1 cup of mushrooms, diced
- 2 cups of carrots, diced
- 2 cups of kale, chopped
- ½ cup of barley, uncooked
- 8 garlic cloves, sliced
- 2 teaspoons of balsamic vinegar
- ½ cup of white wine vinegar
- 6 cups of low sodium beef or vegetable stock
- 1 tablespoon of dried sage
- 1 tablespoon of dried oregano
- 1 tablespoon of dried parsley
- 1 tablespoon of dried rosemary
- 3 teaspoons of black pepper

Directions

1. Preheat your oven to 400 degrees Fahrenheit.

2. Place your beef stew in a roasting pan. Roast your meat 10-15 minutes on each side in the oven, until it is browned. Remove from the oven and set it to the side.

3. Combine your onions, celery, tomatoes, potatoes, sweet potatoes, mushrooms, carrots, and kale in a large stockpot with the canola oil. Sauté until they have browned, around 10 or so minutes.

4. Add the barley and cook for a further 5 minutes. Turn off the heat.

5. Add your beef to the stockpot, along with the balsamic vinegar, white wine vinegar, stock, sage, parsley, oregano, rosemary, and black pepper.

6. Turn the heat back up to medium-high, and bring the soup to a boil. Once it has reached boiling point, reduce the heat back down to low, and allow it to simmer for at least an hour, or until the barley is fully cooked and the soup has thickened.

This recipe makes 12 servings.

Italian Chicken

This recipe is great, as it can be pared down to individual servings quite easily. Double or triple the recipe to make a family meal or make a single serving for when you are wanting something quick to make.

Ingredients

- 3 skinless, boneless chicken breasts (around 3 ounces)
- 1 ½ cups of potatoes, diced
- ¾ cup of onion, diced
- 1 ½ cups of zucchini, diced
- ¾ cup of mushrooms, sliced
- ¾ cup of carrots, sliced
- 1 teaspoon of dried garlic
- 1 teaspoon of dried basil
- 1 teaspoon of dried rosemary
- 1 teaspoon of dried oregano
- 1 teaspoon of dried thyme
- Olive oil

Directions

1. Preheat the oven to 350 degrees Fahrenheit.
2. Using either aluminum foil or parchment paper, cut off three, 12-inch sheets. Fold each in half, and then spread it out and spray the

entire thing with cooking spray (all 3). Place each on their own cookie tray.

3. Mix the garlic, basil, rosemary, oregano, and thyme in a small bowl and set to the side. Place the chicken breasts in a bowl, coat them in olive oil and half of the herb mixture.

4. Place a chicken breast on each piece of foil. Cover the chicken breasts with the potatoes, onion, zucchini, mushrooms, and carrots. Sprinkle the rest of the herb mixture on top of the vegetables.

5. Fold each side of the aluminum foil to create a seal, and then twist the ends to make sure that no liquid escapes the packet. Place on a cookie tray or cookie sheet and put it in the oven.

6. Bake for 40 minutes, or until the chicken is tender.

This recipe makes 3 servings.

Pork Tenderloin with Apples

Substitute the white wine for unsweetened apple juice to make this recipe more kid-friendly.

Ingredients
- 2 pounds of pork tenderloin

- 1 teaspoon of black pepper
- 2 teaspoons of white pepper
- ½ teaspoon of cayenne pepper
- 2 teaspoons of paprika
- 2 apples, sliced
- 1 cup of white wine
- Canola oil

Directions

1. Preheat your oven to 350 degrees Fahrenheit.
2. Trim your tenderloin as desired.
3. In a small bowl, mix the black pepper, white pepper, cayenne, and paprika together. Coat your tenderloin in the spices.
4. In a skillet, add canola oil to the pan over medium-high heat. Sear both sides of the meat, until dark brown.
5. Once seared, place the tenderloin into a roasting pan, and then roast for 30 minutes, or until the internal temperature is 155 degrees Fahrenheit.
6. Once removed from the oven, put the tenderloin on a serving dish and cover with foil to rest for at least 20 minutes.
7. Add the juices and any bits of tenderloin from the bottom of the roasting pan, back to the saucepan you used to cook the tenderloin with, as well as the apples.

8. Sautee the apples until they are browned, add the wine, and reduce the heat to a simmer. Simmer until the wine-stock is reduced and slightly thickened.

9. Serve the apples with the sliced pork and sauce.

This recipe makes 8 servings.

Stuffed Sweet Peppers

Roast your bell peppers before preparing this meal to add an extra layer of flavor.

Ingredients
- 8 green or red bell peppers
- 2 tablespoons of olive oil
- 2 green bell peppers, chopped
- 1 white onion, diced
- 5 cups of corn (if frozen, thaw first)
- 1 teaspoon of chili powder
- 2 tablespoons of fresh cilantro, chopped
- 2 tablespoons of fresh parsley, chopped
- 6 egg whites
- 1 cup of water
- 1 cup of skim milk

Directions

1. Preheat the oven to 350 degrees Fahrenheit.

2. Coat a baking dish with cooking spray and set it to the side.

3. To prepare the bell peppers, slice the tops off and remove the seeds. Be careful not to remove the bottoms. Place the prepared bell peppers in the baking dish and set it to the side.

4. Using a medium skillet, add olive oil and heat over medium-high heat. Add the corn, chopped green peppers, and onion to the skillet and sauté for about 5 minutes, or until the onions are translucent.

5. Add the parsley, cilantro, and chili powder. Reduce the heat and stir.

6. Meanwhile, in a bowl, mix the egg whites and milk together. Once evenly mixed, add it to the corn-pepper mix and turn the heat to medium-high. Stir the two together continuously, until it sets. This new mixture should be moist, not completely dried out.

7. Fill each hollowed-out bell pepper with the corn-milk mix.

8. Pour the water in the bottom of the baking dish and then cover the dish with aluminum foil. Bake for about 15 minutes, or until the peppers have softened.

This recipe makes 8 servings.

Ginger Chicken Stir Fry

Add an Asian inspired flair to a relatively simple meal. To make this dish come together faster, chop the vegetables ahead of time.

Ingredients

- 2 pounds of skinless, boneless chicken breasts, cut into bite-sized pieces
- 2 red bell peppers, sliced
- 2 yellow bell peppers, sliced
- 2 white onions, chopped roughly
- 1 large eggplant, peeled and diced
- 6 green onion stalks, sliced
- 3 garlic cloves
- 2 tablespoons of fresh ginger, minced (or ginger paste)
- 1 ½ cups of chicken stock, low or no sodium
- 4 tablespoons of low sodium soy sauce
- 4 tablespoons of fresh mint, chopped
- ½ cup of fresh basil, chopped
- 4 tablespoons of olive oil, separated

Directions

1. Using a food processor, add the mint, basil, ½ of the stock, green onions, ginger, and

garlic cloves. Pulse the mixture together until it is minced, but not completely pureed together. Set to the side.

2. Using a large skillet, add 2 tablespoons of olive oil to the skillet over medium-high heat. Sauté the yellow onions, bell peppers, and eggplant until they are softened, around 7 minutes. Move to a bowl and cover to keep warm.

3. Add the rest of the olive oil to the skillet, keep it over medium-high heat and add the basil-ginger mixture. Sauté it, stirring constantly so it doesn't stick or burn for at least 1 minute.

4. Add the chicken and soy sauce and sauté until the chicken is mostly cooked around 5-8 minutes. Add the rest of the chicken stock, and bring it to a boil. Then add the vegetable mixture and heat for another 2 minutes.

5. Garnish with sliced green onion and enjoy.

This recipe makes 8 servings.

Couscous Salad

If you find yourself pressed for time, buy "instant couscous", which can be made by boiling water and pouring it over the couscous for 10 minutes.

Ingredients

- 1 cup of couscous
- 1 cup of zucchini, sliced
- 1 yellow bell pepper, sliced
- 1 cup of red onion, diced
- 1 teaspoon of black pepper
- 1 teaspoon of cumin
- 3 teaspoons of lemon juice
- 1 tablespoon of fresh parsley, chopped
- 1 tablespoon of fresh oregano, chopped

Directions

1. Cook the couscous according to its directions.
2. After it is cooked, make sure you mix it gently to fluff it out. Place it in a covered dish. Add in onion, zucchini, bell pepper, cumin, and black pepper. Set this dish aside for the moment.
3. Mix together the lemon juice and olive oil in a small dish. Add the fresh parsley and oregano. Mix this with the couscous-vegetable mixture and place it in the refrigerator to cool.
4. Chill at least 30 minutes before serving.

This recipe makes 8 servings.

Chapter 8: Low Salt Recipes That Will Save You Time

Side Dishes

Slow Cooker Potatoes with Green Beans

This side dish can also be turned into a main dish with the addition of your favorite protein or extra additions to the recipe, such as extra potatoes, carrots, or sweet potatoes.

Ingredients
- 2 pounds of fresh green beans, trimmed and rinsed (if frozen, thaw before using)
- 1 large white onion, sliced
- 1 pound of red potatoes, quartered
- 1 tablespoon of onion powder
- 1 tablespoon of garlic powder
- 2 teaspoons of salt
- 1 tablespoon of black pepper
- 1 cup of low or no-sodium chicken stock (or vegetable stock, if you prefer)

Directions

1. In your crockpot, add the green beans and onion. Add the chicken stock and if the stock does not cover the vegetables, then add just enough water to do so.
2. Add the onion powder, garlic powder, salt, and black pepper and mix gently.
3. Cover the crockpot and allow it to cook on high until the broth begins to boil. Reduce the heat down to low and then allow it to cook for 2 hours.
4. After the 2 hours are up, add the quartered potatoes and allow it to cook for another 40 minutes, or until the potatoes are tender.

This recipe makes 9 servings.

Spaghetti Squash

If you are seeking a replacement for pasta, this is a perfect, low calorie fit for your needs.

Ingredients
- 2 spaghetti squash, seeded and halved
- 4 tablespoons of unsalted butter
- 2 teaspoons of black pepper
- 1 teaspoon of salt

- 2 teaspoons of cumin

Directions

1. Preheat your oven to 375 degrees Fahrenheit.
2. Get a large glass baking dish or tray. Place your spaghetti squash halves inside the dish, with the cut sides facing up.
3. Mix the black pepper, salt, and cumin together in a small bowl, then sprinkle the seasonings on top of the squash equally. Divide the tablespoons of butter between each of the squash.
4. Put the squash in the oven and bake for about 50 minutes or until your fork can easily pierce the flesh of the squash. Use a fork to shred the squash from the skin, and remove to a bowl.
5. Top with your favorite sauce or eat plain.
6. If you want to make a sweet version of this dish, swap the herbs for 2 tablespoons of cinnamon, 4 teaspoons of ground cloves, 2 teaspoons of nutmeg, 2 teaspoons of allspice to sprinkle on top of the squash. Bake for the same amount of time, with the same amount of butter and shred. Add 2 tablespoons of brown sugar to the shredded squash and enjoy.

This recipe makes 8 servings.

Homemade Hash Browns

This is a really rewarding and delicious recipe that can be a lot of fun to make. Shred the potatoes beforehand and store them in water to save time.

Ingredients
- 4 medium potatoes, shredded (your favorite brand works here)
- 1 medium yellow onion, chopped
- ½ cup of flour
- 1 teaspoon of salt
- 2 teaspoons of pepper
- 2 eggs
- Oil, to fry with

Directions
1. Shred your potatoes with a cheese grater. Afterward, place them in a bowl and rinse in cool water until the water becomes clear. Drain the potatoes and squeeze them dry in a cheesecloth, or any other thin cloth that you have. If you do not have any suitable cloth, you can always use a paper towel.
2. Mix the shredded potato with the flour, egg, and onion in a separate bowl.
3. Cover the bottom of a large skillet in oil, and heat it over medium-high heat. When the oil

begins to crackle (check for this by flicking drops of water onto the skillet), place your shredded potatoes all on the bottom of the skillet to form a single layer. If you have enough time, you can also make individual cakes.

4. Cook each side for about 5 minutes, or until browned. If you are cooking the hash browns in a single layer, quarter the hash brown for easy flipping.

5. Once the hash browns have been cooked, remove and place on a plate or tray covered in paper towels to allow the oil to drain. Sprinkle with salt and black pepper. Serve hot.

This recipe makes 8 servings.

Peanut-Carrot Rice

If you are tired of eating the same old plain white rice or wild rice, this can be a great variation to your meals.

Ingredients
- 2 cups of basmati rice
- ½ cup of peanuts, roasted
- 1 medium white onion, thinly sliced

- 1 ½ cups of carrots, grated
- 2 teaspoons of ginger, minced (or ginger paste)
- 2 tablespoons of unsalted butter
- 1 teaspoon of salt
- 1 teaspoon of white pepper
- 1 teaspoon of cayenne pepper
- 4 cups of water
- Fresh cilantro, chopped, optional

Directions

1. In a medium-sized saucepan, cook the rice and water together by bringing to a boil on high heat. Reduce the heat to medium-low, then cover and cook for about 20 minutes, checking to make sure the rice is tender.

2. If you do not buy pre-roasted peanuts, preheat your oven to 350 degrees Fahrenheit. Make sure your peanuts are clean (rinse them under cool water after shelling them), and then place your raw peanuts on a covered tray and put them in the oven. Bake them for about 25 to 30 minutes, and then allow them to cool.

3. Grind the roasted peanuts in a food processor until they are not quite minced. Place these in a bowl and set aside for now.

4. Get a skillet and melt the unsalted butter over medium heat. Add the onion and cook until it is browned, for about 8 to 10 minutes.

5. Add the carrots, ginger, salt, and white pepper. Reduce the heat and cover it to cook for another 5 minutes. Add the cayenne and peanuts, stirring in evenly.

6. When the rice is finished cooking, add it to the skillet, making sure to mix it completely. Top with fresh cilantro and serve.

This recipe makes 12 servings.

Sweet Potatoes

This is a mainstay that can be slightly sweetened to be enjoyed as a side dish or extra sweetened to enjoyed as a dessert. Either are equally enjoyable.

Ingredients

- 3 ⅓ cups of sweet potatoes, boiled and mashed
- ¼ cup of flour
- 8 tablespoons of unsalted butter
- ¼ cup of milk
- 1 egg, beaten
- 1 teaspoon of salt
- 2 tablespoons of sugar

Directions

1. Preheat your oven to 350 degrees Fahrenheit. Coat a glass baking dish in cooking spray.

2. Boil your sweet potatoes and place them in a large bowl. Mash them, and then add the flour, eggs, milk, butter, salt, and sugar.

3. Place in the glass baking dish, making sure to spread it evenly so that the mixture touches all four corners and bake in the oven for 25 minutes, or until slightly browned.

4. To make a more dessert-like version, prepare the sweet potatoes as before, in a bowl, but then add 2 teaspoons of vanilla, ¾ cup of brown sugar, and ½ cup of roughly chopped pecans. Mix together and bake.

This recipe makes 12 servings.

Crispy Zucchini and Potatoes

Enjoy this recipe as a new variation to your neighborhood barbecues.

Ingredients

- 4 medium zucchini, roughly chopped
- 8 medium potatoes, peeled and quartered
- 2 yellow bell peppers, seeded and sliced
- 2 garlic cloves, thinly sliced

- 1 cup of bread crumbs, dried
- 1 tablespoon of black pepper
- 1 tablespoon of paprika
- 4 teaspoons of onion powder
- 2 teaspoons of salt
- ½ cup of olive oil

Directions

1. Preheat your oven to 400 degrees Fahrenheit.
2. In a large bowl, add the zucchini, potatoes, bell peppers, and garlic cloves, along with your breadcrumbs, olive oil, black pepper, paprika, onion powder, and salt. Mix together until the vegetables are evenly coated. Place the vegetable mixture in a large roasting pan.
3. Bake for 60 minutes in the oven, stirring even 20 minutes to ensure that the vegetables brown evenly.

This recipe makes 12 servings.

Sweetened Carrots

You can change the level of sweetness in this recipe depending on your preference, so don't be afraid to tinker with it.

Ingredients

- 32 ounces of carrots (baby carrots would be fine and less work)
- 1 cup of unsalted butter
- 6 tablespoons of honey
- 6 tablespoons of brown sugar

Directions

1. Fill a large pot up to ¾ full of water and add the carrots. Cover them, turn the heat on high, and bring to a boil. This should take about 15 minutes altogether, but cook until the carrots are tender.
2. Drain the carrots and then quickly cover them up back in the pot for another 2 minutes to steam cook.
3. Grab a new pot and turn the heat to medium-low, adding the butter to melt. Once it is melted, add the honey and brown sugar until it is melted and mixed into the butter.
4. Add the carrots and stir to coat them evenly. Cook for another 5 minutes and serve hot.

This recipe makes 8 servings.

Creamed Corn

This recipe often gets a bad rap because of its saltiness straight out of the can. If you enjoy eating creamed corn, here is a perfect opportunity to learn how to make it for yourself and control the salt level.

Ingredients
- 16 ounces of corn kernels (if frozen, thaw before using)
- 8 ounces of plain cream cheese
- ½ cup of milk
- ¼ cup of unsalted butter, melted
- 2 teaspoons of sugar
- 1 teaspoon of salt
- 2 teaspoons of black pepper

Directions
1. In a large bowl, mix the corn, cream cheese, milk, butter, sugar, salt, and black pepper.
2. If you cook it in a crockpot, you can simply put it in the crockpot on high for 2 to 3 hours, or on low for 5 to 6 hours.
3. If you cook the creamed corn on the stove, put it in a large pot on medium-high heat until it begins to boil. Stir gently, then reduce the heat to low, and cover. Cook for the next 1 to

2 hours, stirring gently every 30 minutes until thickened.

This recipe makes 12 servings.

Mashed Potatoes with a Twist

Beef up this old mainstay with your favorite veggie sides!

Ingredients

- 1 pound of yellow potatoes, peeled and quartered
- 1 pound of red potatoes, peeled and quartered
- 12 ounces of carrots, peeled and chopped into bite-sized pieces (use baby carrots to save time)
- 10 ounces of corn kernels, thawed
- 4 garlic cloves
- 1 jalapeno pepper, sliced (optional, or your favorite spicy pepper)
- ¼ cup unsalted butter
- ½ cup of cheddar cheese, shredded
- 1 tablespoon of black pepper
- 2 teaspoons of salt

Directions

1. In a large pot, fill it ¾ full of water, and add the yellow potatoes, red potatoes, pepper, carrots, and garlic. Bring to a boil and boil for 15 minutes, or until the potatoes and carrots are cooked through. Drain the water.
2. Using a potato masher, mash the potatoes and carrots together, and then mix in the butter and corn until the butter is melted and completely mixed in.
3. Add the cheese, black pepper, and salt. Serve while still hot.

This recipe makes 10 servings.

Onion Rice

This simple rice side dish can be paired with any protein you choose and is perfect to bring to potlucks or holiday parties.

Ingredients

- 2 cups of white rice
- 2 small red onions, diced
- 4 cups of reduced-sodium or no-sodium chicken broth
- 2 teaspoons of black pepper
- 1 tablespoon of dried parsley

- 2 tablespoons of olive oil

Directions

1. Add the oil to a large saucepan and turn the heat to medium-high. Heat the oil, and reduce the heat to medium.
2. Add the onion. Sauté the onion until it is translucent, around 5 minutes.
3. Add the rice, taking care to stir it until it is completely coated in the olive oil. Stir until the rice begins to brown.
4. Once the rice begins to brown, add the broth, black pepper, and dried parsley. Bring the liquid to a boil and then cover it and reduce the heat.
5. Simmer for 15 to 20 minutes, until the rice is tender. Serve hot.

This recipe makes 12 servings.

Sugar Snap Peas

Switch up your main side dish and substitute peas for this sweet addition!

Ingredients

- 1 pound of sugar snap peas, rinsed
- 1 small shallot, chopped

- 4 teaspoons of fresh thyme, chopped (or 2 teaspoons of dried thyme)
- 2 teaspoons of salt
- 1 teaspoon of black pepper
- 2 tablespoons of olive oil

Directions

1. Preheat your oven to 450 degrees Fahrenheit.
2. In a mixing bowl, add the sugar snap peas, shallots, and olive oil. Toss to coat the peas evenly with the oil.
3. Spread the sugar snap peas and shallots over a covered cookie tray in an even layer, and then sprinkle the salt and black pepper over the vegetables.
4. Place in the oven and bake for 7 to 8 minutes, or until the peas are cooked. They should still be firm, so beware of overbaking.

This recipe makes 8 servings.

Cucumber Salad

This fresh salad is an interesting and spicy addition to your new menu.

Ingredients
- 5 cucumbers, thinly sliced

- 1 purple onion, thinly sliced
- ¾ cup of sugar
- 1 cup of white vinegar
- ½ cup of water
- 3 teaspoons of dried dill

Directions

1. In a large covered serving bowl, add the cucumbers and onion together.
2. Meanwhile, in a medium saucepan, add the vinegar, sugar, and water and mix together. Place it over medium-high heat and bring to a rolling boil.
3. Once your mixture reaches a rolling boil, immediately take it off the heat and pour over your cucumber-onion mix. Mix it all together so that the cucumbers and onions are evenly coated, and then sprinkle the dill over the top.
4. Cover the mixture and place in the refrigerator to cool for at least 60 minutes before eating. You can eat this salad at room temperature, but it does need to marinate for 60 minutes.

This recipe makes 8 servings.

Scalloped Potatoes

Enjoy a low salt version of this family favorite!

Ingredients
- 3 pounds of yellow potatoes, thinly sliced
- 9 tablespoons of flour
- 7 tablespoons of unsalted butter, divided
- 1 quart of whole milk
- 2 teaspoons of salt
- 1 tablespoon of black pepper

Directions
1. Preheat your oven to 425 degrees Fahrenheit.
2. Coat a large baking dish in cooking spray.
3. Gather your ingredients. Lay down a single layer of potatoes on the bottom of the baking dish, then sprinkle 3 tablespoons of flour, ⅓ of the salt, ⅓ of the pepper, and 2 tablespoons of butter on top of the potatoes.
4. Continue the layers two more times, or until all of the potatoes have been used.
5. Pour the milk over the potatoes until most of the potatoes have been covered with milk, or until about ¾ of the dish has been covered.
6. Place the dish in the oven and bake until the milk begins to boil (this will take around 15 to 20 minutes). Immediately turn the heat down

to 375 degrees Fahrenheit and bake for another 40 to 60 minutes, or until the potatoes are completely cooked.

7. Serve hot.

This recipe makes 8 servings.

Lime Rice

Enjoy this TexMex inspired side dish!

Ingredients
- 2 cups of white rice
- 4 cups of water
- 2 tablespoons of unsalted butter
- 2 tablespoons of lime zest
- 4 tablespoons of lime juice
- 1 cup of fresh cilantro, chopped

Directions
1. If you have a rice cooker, cook the rice according to its directions. Otherwise, in a medium-sized pot, add the rice and water, and bring to a boil. Once the water is boiling, cover and reduce the heat to low heat, and allow the rice to simmer for the next 20 minutes, or until the rice is fully cooked. Add

liquid if the rice absorbs all of the liquid and is still crunchy.

2. Once the rice is cooked, add the lime zest, lime juice, butter, and fresh cilantro. Mix evenly and serve.

This recipe makes 8 servings.

Main Dishes

Round Roast

Use this cooking technique any time you have to cook with a tough piece of meat. This technique makes any tough, cheap cut of meat tender and flavorful.

Ingredients
- 3-pound beef roast
- 2 tablespoons of minced garlic (or garlic paste)
- 1 tablespoon of dried parsley
- 1 tablespoon of dried rosemary
- 1 tablespoon of dried basil
- 1 tablespoon of pepper
- 1 teaspoon of salt

- 3 tablespoons of olive oil

Directions

1. Preheat your oven to 500 degrees Fahrenheit.
2. In a separate bowl, mix together the parsley, rosemary, basil, pepper, and salt. Take a smaller bowl, and mix together the olive oil and garlic.
3. Mix the garlic and herb mixtures together to form a paste. Rub it all over the roast.
4. Place the roast in a baking dish or roasting pan. Place in the oven. Immediately, reduce the heat to 475 degrees Fahrenheit. Roast the beef for 20 minutes and then turn the oven off. Let the roast sit in the oven for 3 hours. Do not open the oven door to check the roast.
5. Remove the roast and check that the internal temperature of the roast is at least 145 degrees Fahrenheit.

This recipe makes 6 servings.

Balsamic Lamb Chops

This recipe is a great way to use your favorite herbs to flavor the chops. Mix and match to switch up the recipe!

Ingredients
- 8 lamb chops
- ½ cup of shallots, minced
- ⅔ cup of balsamic vinegar
- 1 ½ cups of reduced or no-sodium chicken broth
- 2 tablespoons of olive oil
- 2 tablespoons of unsalted butter
- 3 teaspoons of dried rosemary
- 2 teaspoons of dried thyme
- 2 teaspoons of dried basil
- 3 teaspoons of white pepper
- 2 teaspoons of salt

Directions
1. Mix together the rosemary, thyme, basil, pepper, and salt in a small bowl. Rub the herb mixture onto the lamb chops and place on a plate or cookie tray. Cover them for 30 minutes to help the meat absorb the flavor.
2. Take a large skillet and heat the olive oil over medium-high heat. Cook the lamb chops for

about 5 minutes on each side, depending on how cooked you enjoy your meat. 5 minutes on each side will give you medium doneness. As they are cooked, place them on a plate and cover them to keep warm.

3. Do not remove the skillet from the heat. Sauté the shallots for 2 to 3 minutes, or until they are translucent and then add the vinegar and chicken broth.

4. Stir the mixture, taking care to scrape up any lamb or herbs that have been left on the bottom of the skillet, for the next 5 to 6 minutes, until the liquid has been reduced by half and has thickened. After this, remove from the heat and add the butter.

5. Pour the sauce over your lamb chops and enjoy.

This recipe makes 8 servings.

Lemon Tilapia

Spice up a rather plain protein with strong flavors, such as other citrus fruits or spices. You can sauté, grill, or bake this recipe.

Ingredients
- 8 tilapia fillets
- 2 tablespoons of unsalted butter, melted
- 2 tablespoons of garlic, minced (or garlic paste)
- 6 tablespoons of lemon juice (fresh or bottled)
- 3 teaspoons of dried parsley
- 2 teaspoons of black pepper
- 1 teaspoon of salt

Directions
1. Preheat your oven to 375 degrees Fahrenheit. Use either a baking dish or a cookie tray, spray either with a cooking spray.
2. To prepare your tilapia fillets, make sure you rinse them under cool water when you take them out of the package and then dry them with paper towels.
3. Mix together the parsley, black pepper, and salt in a small bowl. In a separate bowl, mix together the butter, lemon juice, and garlic.

Add the herb mixture to the butter garlic mixture, making sure to mix them evenly.

4. Coat the fillets in the mixture and then place them on the baking dish or cookie tray.

5. Bake for 25 minutes, or until the fish turns white and flakes when you touch the middle with a fork.

This recipe makes 8 servings.

Rosemary Chicken

This is a great recipe for when you need to get dinner in the oven right away. Switch out the chicken thighs for your favorite cuts of meat.

Ingredients
- 8 boneless chicken thighs
- 4 medium red potatoes, quartered (if you use a different type of potatoes, peel them)
- 2 tablespoons of fresh rosemary, chopped (or 1 tablespoon of dried rosemary)
- 1 tablespoon of fresh oregano, chopped (or 2 teaspoons of dried oregano)
- 2 teaspoons of garlic powder
- 2 teaspoons of salt
- 4 teaspoons of black pepper
- ⅓ cup of olive oil

Directions

1. Preheat your oven to 375 degrees.
2. In a separate bowl, mix together the rosemary, oregano, garlic powder, salt, and black pepper. Quarter your potatoes and place them, along with your chicken in a bowl. Coat them in the olive oil and herb mixture. Allow it to rest for 20 minutes.
3. Place the chicken and potatoes in a large baking dish and place in the oven. Do not cover it.
4. Bake for at least 1 hour. If you want your chicken to be extra crispy, baste every 20 minutes.

This recipe makes 8 servings.

Honey Sweetened Pecan Pork Chops

If you enjoy mixing sweet and savory elements in your food, you won't be disappointed with this dish!

Ingredients

- 2 ½ pounds of boneless pork loin, pounded flat
- 1 cup of flour
- 2 teaspoons of cumin

- 1 tablespoon of black pepper
- 2 teaspoons of salt
- ½ cup of honey
- ½ cup of pecans, roughly chopped
- 2 tablespoons of olive oil

Directions

1. In a separate bowl, mix together the flour, cumin, black pepper, and salt. Coat both sides of the boneless pork loin in this flour mixture.
2. In a medium-sized skillet, add the olive oil and heat to medium-high heat. Fry the pork loin for about 5 minutes on each side, until it browns or reaches the desired doneness. Place the pork loin into a covered dish to keep warm.
3. Without removing the skillet from the heat, add the pecans and honey to the skillet. Stir the honey, pecans, and pan drippings together, making sure to scrape any bits off the bottom of the pan. Stir until it is heated through.
4. Serve the pork loin with the sauce.

This recipe makes 8 servings.

Garlic Shrimp

This recipe is deceptively simple, yet one of the tastiest things you can make all year. This is perfect for last-minute guests or a quick bite to eat.

Ingredients

- 1 pound of shrimp, deveined and peeled (if frozen, thaw before using)
- 1 pound of pasta (use your favorite, but we recommend linguine)
- 1 tablespoon of unsalted butter
- 4 garlic cloves, minced (or 3 tablespoons of garlic paste)
- 4 tablespoons of white wine
- 1 tablespoon of parmesan, grated
- 2 teaspoons of fresh parsley, chopped
- 2 teaspoons of black pepper
- 1 teaspoon of salt

Directions

1. Bring a large pot of water to boil and add the pasta to the water. Cook for 7 to 10 minutes, until the pasta is cooked al dente. Drain immediately.
2. Melt the butter in a medium saucepan over medium heat, then add the cheese, garlic, wine, parsley, salt, and pepper. Reduce the

heat to low, and then simmer for 5 minutes. Stir often, making sure that nothing gets stuck to the bottom of the pan.

3. Add the shrimp to the saucepan and increase the heat back to medium-high heat. Cook the shrimp for about 5 minutes, or until the shrimp starts to go pink.

4. Divide the pasta between servings and top with the shrimp sauce. If you want, add more parmesan cheese and top with fresh parsley.

This recipe makes 8 servings.

Gnocchi

Making traditional Italian food can seem a bit tricky and intimidating. If you are interested in eating other Italian cuisines outside of spaghetti and pizza, gnocchi is a great recipe to start with.

Ingredients

- 4 potatoes (we recommend Yukon Gold or red)
- 2 eggs
- 4 cups of flour

Directions

1. Peel your potatoes and rough chop them for boiling. Fill a large pot of water about ¾ of the way full of water; add 2 teaspoons of salt, and bring to a boil.

2. Add the potatoes and boil them under the potatoes are tender, but still firm enough to hold their shape. This will take about 15 minutes. Drain the pot, allow the potatoes to cool and then mash them.

3. Once you have mashed your potatoes, take a large bowl and add the potatoes in them, along with the flour and egg. Mix thoroughly, and then knead until the potato mixture forms into a ball.

4. Pour the dough out onto a floured tabletop. Divide the dough into sections, and then shape those sections into long, narrow "snakes".

5. Slice the snakes into ½ inch pieces. Get another large pot, fill it ¾ of the way full of water, add 1 teaspoon of salt, and bring it to a boil.

6. Add your gnocchi balls to the boiling water and cook them for around 5 minutes, or until they begin to rise to the top of the water. Drain the water and serve either plain or with

your favorite low salt cheese or marinara sauce.

This recipe makes 8 servings.

Chicken Breasts with Apple Stuffing

Tired of making pie? Use up your extra apples in this delicious recipe and see if you have a new favorite. The apples keep the chicken breast moist and tender inside and out.

Ingredients
- 4 skinless, boneless chicken breasts
- 1 cup of apple, chopped in bite-sized pieces
- 4 tablespoons of cheddar cheese, shredded
- 2 teaspoons of dried basil
- 2 teaspoons of dried oregano
- 2 teaspoons of dried parsley
- 1 teaspoon of dried rosemary
- 1 teaspoon of black pepper
- 1 teaspoon of salt
- 2 tablespoons of plain dried bread crumbs
- 3 teaspoons of cornstarch
- ½ cup white wine
- 1 tablespoon of unsalted butter
- ½ cup of water
- 2 tablespoons of water

156

Directions

1. In a medium-sized bowl, combine the apple, breadcrumbs, cheese, basil, parsley, rosemary, black pepper, and salt together.

2. Pound the chicken breasts flat and divide the apple-breadcrumb mixture evenly between the chicken breasts. Fold the chicken breasts over the mixture, and secure it with toothpicks. You can also use store-bought twine to tie them together.

3. Place a skillet on medium-high heat and melt the butter. Transfer the chicken breasts to the skillet and brown on both sides, around 5 minutes on each side. Add the wine and ½ cup of water. Cover the skillet, reduce the heat to medium-low, and cook the chicken for around 20 minutes.

4. Once the chicken is cooked, move it to a serving dish. In a different bowl, mix the cornstarch and 2 tablespoons of water. Add this to the juices leftover in the skillet. Cook over medium-high heat until it thickens and begins to boil.

5. Slice the chicken breasts in half. Add the gravy to the chicken breasts and serve.

This recipe makes 8 servings.

Mushroom Soup

Try this creamy soup with your favorite mushrooms!

Ingredients

- 2 cups of portobello mushrooms, chopped
- 2 cups of shiitake mushrooms, chopped
- ½ cup of unsalted butter
- 4 shallots, chopped
- 10 ounces of low sodium chicken broth
- 2 cups of half and half
- 4 tablespoons of flour
- 1 tablespoon of black pepper
- 2 teaspoons of salt
- ¼ teaspoon of ground cinnamon

Directions

1. In a large saucepan, melt the butter with medium-high heat. Add the portobello, shiitake mushrooms, and shallots to the butter, sauté for 5 to 10 minutes until the mushrooms and shallots are softened and translucent.
2. Add the flour, taking care to coat the mushrooms and shallots as evenly as you can.
3. Add the chicken broth, and stir for another 5 minutes, until the mixture thickens and begins to boil.

4. Add the half and half, making sure that it completely mixes in with the broth, and then add the salt, black pepper, and ground cinnamon. Reduce the heat and allow it to simmer for another 5 minutes. Serve immediately.

This recipe makes 8 servings.

Asparagus Chicken Penne

Incorporate fresh asparagus into this light, well-flavored chicken dish!

Ingredients
- 2 boneless, skinless chicken breasts, chopped into bite-sized pieces
- 16 ounces of penne pasta
- 1 tablespoon of minced garlic (or garlic paste)
- 1 bunch of asparagus, trimmed into bite-sized pieces
- ⅓ cup of low sodium chicken broth
- ⅓ cup parmesan cheese
- 6 tablespoons of olive oil
- 1 tablespoon of black pepper
- 1 tablespoon of onion powder
- 2 teaspoons of salt

Directions

1. Prepare the penne pasta according to the directions e.g. bring a large pot of water to boil, add the pasta, and cook until tender, around 8 to 10 minutes. Drain immediately.

2. In a small bowl, mix the garlic, onion powder, black pepper, and salt together. In a large mixing bowl coat the chicken breasts with the garlic mixture evenly.

3. Using a large skillet, add half of the olive oil to the skillet and bring to medium-high heat.

4. Cook the chicken on the heated skillet until it is browned on the sides, around 5 minutes each. Place the chicken on paper towels to drain the oil.

5. Do not take the skillet off the heat, but add the chicken broth. Stir slightly and see if you can unstick any chicken bits from the bottom of the pan.

6. Add the asparagus and more salt and pepper. Mix it around to coat the asparagus, and then cover for 5 to 10 minutes until the asparagus is cooked all the way. Add the chicken and reheat.

7. Once the chicken and asparagus are heated through, add it to the pasta and mix it evenly. Allow it to settle for 10 minutes, and then add 3 tablespoons of olive oil. Top with the parmesan cheese and serve.

This recipe makes 8 servings.

Mexican Supreme Beef

This dish is versatile in that it can be used as a taco filling, or with sides of mashed potatoes or rice.

Ingredients
- 2 pounds of beef stew meat, cubed
- 2 small yellow onions, diced
- 1 tablespoon of garlic, minced (or garlic paste)
- 6 green onions, sliced
- 1 jalapeno pepper, sliced
- 1 tablespoon of dried oregano
- 1 tablespoon of dried rosemary
- 1 tablespoon of dried basil
- 2 teaspoons of black pepper
- 1 teaspoon of salt
- 8 ounces of your favorite low sodium salsa
- ⅓ cup of fresh cilantro, chopped
- Olive oil
- Juice of 1 lime

Directions

1. In a large skillet, add the olive oil and onion to sauté over medium-high heat. Sauté the onion until it is browned.
2. Add the beef stew meat, garlic, rosemary, basil, black pepper, and salt. Make sure it is all mixed together and equally coating the meat as you sauté it.
3. In a separate bowl, add the cilantro, green onion, jalapeno, lime juice, and oregano together. Mix thoroughly, then add to the meat mixture when it is browned.
4. Next, add the salsa and mix thoroughly so that it coats the meat.
5. Cover the skillet and continue cooking it for another 5 to 10 minutes, until the meat is completely cooked. Serve hot.

This recipe makes 8 servings.

Chapter 9: Make a Smart Shopping List and Manage Your Budget

Become a Smart Shopper

Whether you have much experience cooking or not, you are going to spend the rest of your life extensively reading labels and judging whether or not you've delicately balanced the amount of sodium that your body actually needs vs. the actual flavor of the dish you are trying to create. Especially when you are dealing with fresh produce, it can get pricey pretty fast. So, the first thing you will have to learn is how to be a smart shopper.

Make a Budget

This is possibly the most important advice I could give you. Sit down with your finances and figure out exactly what you can devote to your new lifestyle change. Do you need cooking equipment, such as a crockpot, instapot, soup pot, etc.? How much food can you afford to buy each week vs. what you can cook? These questions need to be weighed up delicately and answered with a specifically calculated budget that you do not deviate from, no matter what ("Smart Shopper", 2017).

Buy at the End of the Season

As with everything fun in life, the best products are sometimes the most expensive, and sometimes we can't afford to pay for them. This is where research and patience come in. Say that you enjoy fresh blueberries, but can't afford the tiny, 4-ounce cartons that most grocery stores sell them in. Wait until the end of the growing season and see if they have a special sale, particularly if the berries aren't selling well. Or wait and see if a similar fruit comes up that you could substitute. You won't always be able to buy what you want when you want, but you don't have to walk away empty-handed either ("Smart Shopper", 2017).

Make a List

Behind making a budget, making a list and sticking to it is possibly the most important advice you could ever take away from this eBook. It goes hand in hand with creating your budget. Do not deviate from your list because of an impulse buy. You don't need that unapproved food item. It will more than likely be there the next time you go to the store. Take the time, if you really want it, to budget it into your meal plan for the next week. Be wholly responsible and in control of your actions ("Smart Shopper", 2017).

How to Budget

If you have never had to create a budget before, it can seem overwhelming at first. Particularly when you are going from buying groceries in the short term to long term, bulk buying. Your first step should be to figure out exactly what your budget is— what you can afford to spend on groceries alone ("Successful Budget", n.d.).

How well do you cook? Do you know how to reasonably cook more difficult proteins like lamb, or tougher cuts of meat that would require more work put into them to make them taste delicious?

How much time do you have to grocery shop and cook? Do you work over forty hours a week? Perhaps you want to invest in a crockpot so that you can make quick, easy meals to throw in your crockpot, set it on low, and forget about it until you get home later that night. Are you always traveling? Perhaps you want to make several casseroles and soups that you can freeze and then throw in the oven whenever you come home.

These questions and your answers to them will determine the types of proteins and produce that you buy. If you travel often and are gone for days at a time, then it doesn't make sense for you to waste money on fresh produce that will rot in your refrigerator. Save your money and buy frozen vegetables and freeze your proteins after buying (or buy frozen).

Once you have determined your budget, factor in other considerations. You have your budget—now where can you find a deal? Or is it worth it to find deals to you, in terms of time and money? This is where quality over quantity comes from. If you need to invest in cookware, then is it worth you spending extra money on something that will make your life easier and infinitely less stressful, as well as last for several years? For some people, the answer is yes. Others will go a different, equally valid direction.

The most important aspect of determining and managing your budget is to stick to it. So, there is no such thing as an "impulse" buy because you plan and budget for every ounce of food that you make. You decide when you are going to indulge yourself in a low to no salt roast beef sandwich with all of the roasted peppers and onions, instead of going to the guy in the cart down the street and buying a sandwich covered in salt and extra grease. Your budget is yours to do as you will. Just follow it explicitly and do not make excuses for yourself.

Chapter 10: Challenges and Solutions for You and Your Family

When you decide to embark upon a lifestyle change, everyone that is involved in your life is involved in that lifestyle change as well. Your parents, your friends, your partner, your children—they are all subject to anything and everything that you do. When you decide to embark upon a change in the way that you eat, you automatically take yourself out of the count for most dishes at restaurants, and even at the homes of friends and family. Most restaurant dishes are full of excess sodium and added salt, as well as grease. While some friends and family may embrace your new reduced to no added sodium or salt diet, others may not feel the same way. It is more than likely not done in a malicious way, but the truth of it is that sometimes "special diets" wreak more havoc during holiday dinners than unruly children.

The best way to face these challenges together as friends, as family, is to be as open about it as possible. Don't hide your reasons for why you have decided to eliminate or mostly reduce added sodium and salt in your diet. Explain in detail as to how your medical condition forced you to make this decision, forced you to change your lifestyle completely. Don't

168

keep it a secret. Be completely open. Education is power, and not only that, but it helps you stand your ground and make plans.

When it comes to your direct family, whether you have a partner, children, or roommates you live with—plan. Don't allow the situation to get out of hand and out of your control. The moment you do not have a plan is the moment you have lost (Jones, Holton, & Jowitt, n.d.). When it comes to grocery shopping—make a plan. Don't go to the store without a list. Involve your family or those closest to you in the planning, and it will work out to be more manageable for everyone involved.

Another thing that helps your family help you take on this new lifestyle change is to involve them in the creation of a schedule (Jones, Holton, & Jowitt, n.d.). If you did not do much cooking before, then cooking will soon have to be squeezed into your schedule regularly. This is not your burden to bear alone. You are not alone—you have your family, your partner, and your children to support you. So, allow them to assist you. Create a new schedule—when you go grocery shopping, who is going to go with you? Who is going to help prepare the vegetables? Who is on dish duty after cooking? Ask your family and arrange the schedule so that it best suits everyone's schedule. Give a little. The whole family will be making these changes with you, and it is not

169

only your life that is being upheaved, in a sense. The best way to keep yourself consistent and on track with your new diet is to make your diet a lifestyle change for the entire family, and not just a *diet*, to be discarded in the short-term.

Remember that no one is perfect, and life isn't perfect. Sometimes things don't go your way. Mistakes will be made. You want to work together as a team. You can't work together as a team if you are visibly angry or upset when something goes wrong (Jones, Holton, & Jowitt, n.d.). They are still learning, and you are still learning—be gentle with yourself and your family. Take everything as it comes. If this is the first time your partner or child has diced onion or the first time they have used more than salt and pepper as a seasoning staple, then don't get upset when they make mistakes. Don't get angry with yourself when you make those same mistakes. You're still learning, and you're trying to learn something that is more than likely utterly foreign to you. There are bound to be some mishaps along the way, and if you approach them with a good attitude and the knowledge that you will eventually find your way, then it can be an enjoyable and rewarding experience for your entire family.

But your family has to know that you are on their side, that you are all still a team. Don't approach meal prep as a particular circle in the seventh hell.

Try to make it fun. Make it a group activity. Depending on your children's ages, they may resent having to add another chore. That is why you should not approach it as a chore. Involve your children and partner in it as much as you can—ask them their opinions, what type of job (cleaning, chopping, mixing, peeling, etc.) do they like the most and what are their favorite dishes. Take their opinions into consideration. Let your partner and children each choose a recipe if they want to, and make it a fun family activity (Jones, Holton, & Jowitt, n.d.). The most crucial point of all this is that you will never overcome any challenges together as a family unless you behave as a family unit and back each other up when you need each other the most. Hopefully, this is the first of many steps in that direction.

Conclusion

It can be hard to take the first step in building yourself a new life, particularly if you have to bring other people with you. Sometimes friends and family can be your biggest hindrance. There is something about food and beverages that makes otherwise lovely and reasonable people act entirely out of character if they feel intimidated or left behind, in the same way that an alcoholic feels threatened by the only person not drinking alcohol at dinner. However, hopefully, with the techniques mentioned in the previous chapter, you can help them see everything from your point of view and what you are trying to accomplish.

Perhaps they are reacting to some sort of insecurity or worry that you are projecting unconsciously. The decision to completely overhaul your diet into a lifestyle change and not into an "I want to lose 10 pounds before my brother gets married" type of diet that is only temporary can bring out exciting reactions, and reactions you may not have expected. Often, it can change how your loved one thought of you or what they believed to be true of you—mainly if you are successful in your new lifestyle change.

If you feel nervous about making too many changes at one time, and you feel as though you will slip up or "relapse," then make small changes first and build your way up. For example, if you usually have scrambled eggs cooked in salted butter and seasoned with salt, pepper, and thyme, along with (salted) buttered toast, switch it up. Decide to make a "Mexican style" scrambled egg breakfast with sautéed green onions with your eggs in olive oil and topped with fresh salsa (diced tomatoes and onions with chopped fresh cilantro and fresh lime or lemon juice) and black beans (drained and rinsed). Or go the other direction and indulge your sweet tooth with some homemade granola with your favorite dried fruits and plain nuts, or a blueberry smoothie bowl made with frozen fruit and oatmeal. You are in charge of your body and your health. Keep your changes consistent and stick to them until you slowly get used to the change that you have implemented from your usual routine. Then make another change and another change and another change—until one day, you find that your whole life has been turned upside down.

One of the easiest ways to keep consistent with the lifestyle changes that you have made is to make them meaningful and essential to you. If you find yourself struggling with slipping into your old ways, find meals that had some meaning to you and make you think of happy memories—and recreate them without all of the excesses of extra sodium and salt. Allow yourself to taste and enjoy your dish and think of your happy memories with your friends and family. Open yourself up to them—about your struggles, your hopes for the future. Make it a family affair all the way. If you can replace your previously half-heartedly salted meals with healthy goals and desires—particularly with your desire to live a healthier lifestyle than before—then nothing will stop you. Go back to your old haunts, your old favorites, in terms of meals and recipes, and give them a new place in a healthier, better you.

Don't push your family away when you feel insecure or unworthy. Let them help you. You have to take the first step forward, which you did in acknowledging that your current health issue(s) could not allow you to continue living the same lifestyle that you had before. You took several more steps in addressing one of the main contributors to your health issue(s) and did the research that led you straight to this eBook. Continue walking ahead—but you don't have to walk alone. Learn how to delegate tasks and be open about your needs, mainly if this is the first time you have ever put your needs to the forefront. Let your family see that you can be vulnerable and that they are needed as well as loved by you.

Lifestyle changes of this magnitude are tricky, especially if this is all new to you. Focus on the positives and everything that you have gained in your life as a result of being proactive and acknowledging the health issue(s) that you are currently dealing with. It may be something that you have to deal with for the rest of your life. How will you choose to deal with it? By ignoring it until it worsens to an undeniable degree and the absolute worst happens, or by making half-hearted changes that help you feel better for a short period and then go right back to your old ways?

No—you have chosen to confront your fears and face the truth straight in the face. I wish you nothing but luck on your journey and hope that these recipes can help you in some small way.

The end... almost!

Reviews are not easy to come by.

As an independent author with a tiny marketing budget, I rely on readers, like you, to leave a short review on Amazon.

Even if it's just a sentence or two!

So if you liked the book, please leave a review.

I am very appreciative for your review as it truly makes a difference.

Thank you from the bottom of my heart for purchasing this book and reading it to the end.

References

"5 Simple Steps to Create a Successful Budget". (n.d.). Retrieved from https://www.payoff.com/life/money/5-simple-steps-to-create-a-successful-budget/

"14 Tips on How to be a Smart Shopper". (August 1, 2017). Retrieved from https://acentsiblegal.com/2017/08/01/how-to-be-a-smart-shopper/

"Acute Kidney Failure". (n.d.). Retrieved from https://www.mayoclinic.org/diseases-conditions/kidney-failure/symptoms-causes/syc-20369048

"Breakfast Recipes". (n.d.). Retrieved from https://www.tasteofhome.com/healthy-eating/low-sodium-recipes/low-sodium-breakfast-recipes/

Day, Allison. (January 4, 2016). "Healthy Eating". Retrieved from https://www.foodnetwork.ca/healthy-eating/photos/healthy-satisfying-low-sodium-snacks

"Diet: a balanced diet and your health". (August 1, 2016). Retrieved from http://i-base.info/guides/side/diet-a-balanced-diet-and-your-health

"Heart Failure". (n.d.). Retrieved from https://www.mayoclinic.org/diseases-conditions/heart-failure/symptoms-causes/syc-20373142

"High Blood Pressure (Hypertension)". (n.d.). Retrieved from https://www.mayoclinic.org/diseases-conditions/high-blood-pressure/symptoms-causes/syc-20373410

"Hyponatremia". (n.d.). Retrieved from https://www.mayoclinic.org/diseases-conditions/hyponatremia/symptoms-causes/syc-20373711

Jones, Pam., Holton, Vicki., & Jowitt, Angela. (n.d.). 6 Common Team Challenges - How to Overcome Them and Grow Your Team. Retrieved from https://www.bytestart.co.uk/tackle-common-team-challenges-develop-team-performance.html

Kubala, Jillian. (December 10, 2018). Low-Sodium Diet: Benefits, Food Lists, Risks, and More. Retrieved from https://www.healthline.com/nutrition/low-sodium-diet

Lewis, James L. (March 2018). Hypernatremia. Retrieved from https://www.merckmanuals.com/professional/endocrine-and-metabolic-disorders/electrolyte-disorders/hypernatremia

"Low Sodium". (n.d.). Retrieved from https://www.gerolsteiner.de/en/water-knowledge/water-lexicon/low-sodium/

"Low Sodium Main Dish". (n.d.). Retrieved from https://www.allrecipes.com/recipes/16972/healthy-recipes/low-sodium/main-dishes/

"Low Sodium Recipes". (n.d.). Retrieved from https://www.mayoclinic.org/healthy-lifestyle/recipes/low-sodium-recipes/rcs-20077197

McBean, Brenda. (October 2, 2017). Everything You Should Know About Hypernatremia. Retrieved from https://www.healthline.com/health/hypernatremia

McCulloch, Marsha. (September 9, 2018). 30 Foods High in Sodium and What To Eat Instead.

Retrieved from https://www.healthline.com/nutrition/foods-high-in-sodium

Mozaffarian, Dariush. (n.d.). What are the Health Benefits of Sodium?. Retrieved from https://www.sharecare.com/health/sodium/what-health-benefits-sodium

"Salt and Sodium". (n.d.). Retrieved from https://www.hsph.harvard.edu/nutritionsource/salt-and-sodium/

"Sodium in Drinking Water". (n.d.). Retrieved from https://www.dhs.wisconsin.gov/water/sodium.htm